Memmo Caporilli

THE POPES
The Ecumenical Councils
The Jubilees - The Holy Years

History and Images

Edition 2003

Euroedit - Trento

The Popes - The Councils - The Jubilees

First edition (1 colour poster) 1949
Second edition (fascicule) 1958
Third edition (black and white poster) 1975
Fourth edition (volume) 1982
Fifth edition (full colour poster) 1986
Sixth edition, expanded (full colour volume) 1999

PREFACE

This book is based on the definitive lists of the Popes and Anti-popes. These lists have been compiled with the most updated historical findings by Monsignor Angelo Mercati, Prefect of the Vatican Archives, and were officially accepted and published, for the first time, by the Holy See in its 1947 Yearbook.

As a result of this research and revision, six Elections have been found to be illegal and two of the Popes have turned out to be the same person. Three new Pontiffs, never mentioned in any of the previous lists, have been confirmed while four of the legitimate Popes have been stripped of their title of Holiness.

Consequently, there are presently 294 medallions in the Patriarchal Basilica of S. Paolo and 18 of them are still empty. After the revision, 16 of the Pope's portraits are no longer in the definitive list of the Roman Supreme Pontiffs, leaving us with 260 legitimate portraits plus two re-elections of Benedict IX and plus Leo VIII and Silvester III legitimated by the last revision.

At the present date, the official count from the Pontifical Annuary is 264.

The number of Anti-popes has finally been confirmed to be thirty-seven.

All modesty aside, this allows us to affirm that this book is, chronologically speaking, the most exact and most updated.

The photographs of the Supreme Pontiffs have been gathered from the "Mosaics of Chronology" that exist in the Roman

Basilica of S. Paolo Fuori le Mura: the oldest and the most complete iconography of the Roman Pontiffs.

Out of pure and simple curiosity for the reader, it is interesting to note that of the 264 Popes (262 to be exact because Pope Benedict IX, during the dreadful medieval fights between Popes and Anti-popes, was elected three times) 205 were Italians of whom 106 were Romans and 57 foreigners, comprise of 19 Frenchmen, 14 Greeks, 8 Syrians, 5 Germans, 3 Africans, 2 Spaniards, 1 Austrian, 1 Palestinian, 1 Englishman, 1 Dutchman and 1 Pole.

M.C.

ON THE VACANCY OF THE APOSTOLIC SEE AND THE ELECTION OF THE ROMAN PONTIFF

Extract from the "Apostolic Constitution" - "Universi Dominici Gregis" dated February 22, 1996

VACANCY OF THE APOSTOLIC SEE

- As soon as he is informed of the death of the Supreme Pontiff, the Camerlengo of Holy Roman Church must officially ascertain the Pope's death, in the presence of the Master of Papal Liturgical Celebrations, the Cleric Prelates of the Apostolic Camera and the Secretary and Chancellor of the same; the latter must draw up the official death certificate. The Camerlengo must also place seals on the Pope's study and bedroom.

- The Cardinal Vicar of Rome must inform the People of Rome by means of a special announcement; all the Cardinals present are to swear an oath to observe the prescriptions and maintain secrecy.

- Next, each Cardinal shall add: *And I, (name) Cardinal (name), so promise, pledge and swear.* and, placing his hand on the Gospels, he will add: *so help me god and these holy gospels which i now touch with my hand.*

- After the death of the Roman Pontiff, the Cardinals celebrate the funeral rites for the repose of his soul for nine consecutive days, in accordance with the *ordo exsequiarum Romani Pontificis.*

- If burial takes place in the Vatican Basilica, the relevant official document is drawn up by the Notary of the Chapter of the Basilica or by the Canon Archivist.

- No one is permitted to use any means whatsoever to photograph or film the Supreme Pontiff either on his sickbed or after death, or record his words for subsequent reproduction.

- After the burial of the Supreme Pontiff and during the election of the new Pope, no part of the private apartment of the Supreme Pontiff is to be lived in.

THE ELECTION OF THE ROMAN PONTIFF

- The right to elect the Roman Pontiff belongs exclusively to the Cardinals of the Holy Roman Church, with the exception of those who have reached their eightieth birthday before the day of the Roman Pontiff's death or the day when the Apostolic See becomes vacant. The maximum number of Cardinal electors must not exceed one hundred and twenty. The right of active election by any other ecclesiastical dignitary or the intervention of any lay power of any level or order is absolutely prohibited.

- The Conclave for the election of the Supreme Pontiff takes place within the territory of Vatican City, in determined areas and buildings, closed to all unauthorized persons in order to ensure suitable accommodation for the Cardinal electors and all those who legitimately called to cooperate.

- The Cardinal electors, from the beginning of the election until its conclusion and the public announcement of its outcome, are not to communicate, either in writing, by telephone or by any other means of communication, with persons outside the area where the election is taking place.

- When the funeral rites for the deceased Pope have been celebrated according to the prescribed ritual, and everything necessary for the regular functioning of the election has been prepared, on the appointed day - on the fifteenth day after the death of the Pope no later than the twentieth - the Cardinal electors shall meet in the Basilica of Saint Peter's in the Vatican. When the last of the Cardinal electors has taken the oath, the Master of Papal Liturgical Celebrations will give the order *Extra Omnes*, and all those not taking part in the Conclave must leave the Sistine Chapel.

- Since the forms of election known as the *Acclamationem seu Inspirationem* and *per compromissum* are abolished, the form of electing the Roman Pontiff shall henceforth be *per scrutinium* alone.

I therefore decree that for the valid election of the Roman Pontiff two thirds of the votes are required, calculated on the basis of the total number of electors present.

- The voting process is carried out in three phases. The first phase, which can be called the pre-scrutiny phase, comprises the preparation and distribution of the ballot papers and the drawing of three Cardinal-Scrutineers.

- The second phase, the scrutiny itself, comprises: 1) the placing of the ballots in the appropriate receptacle; 2) the mixing and counting of the ballots; 3) the opening of the votes. Each Cardinal elector, in order of precedence, having completed and folded his ballot, holds it up so that it can be seen and carries it to the altar, at which the Scrutineers stand and upon which there is placed a receptacle, covered by a plate, for receiving the ballots. Having reached the altar, the Cardinal elector says aloud the following oath:

I call as my witness Christ the lord who will be my judge, that my ote is gi en to the one who before god i think should be elected.

He then places the ballot on the plate which he uses to drop it into the receptacle. Having done this, he bows to the altar and returns to his place.

- After all the ballots of the Cardinal electors have been placed in the receptacle, the first Scrutineer shakes it several times in order to mix them and immediately afterwards the last Scrutineer proceeds to count them.

- When all the ballots have been opened, the Scrutineers add up the sum of the votes obtained by the different names and write them down on a separate sheet of paper. The last Scrutineer, as he reads out the individual ballots, pierces each one with a needle through the word *Eligio* and places it on a thread, so that the ballots can be more securely preserved

- Then follows the third and last phase, also known as the post-scrutiny phase, which comprises: 1) the counting of the votes; 2) the checking of the same; 3) the burning of the ballots.

The Scrutineers add up all the votes that each individual has received and if no one has obtained two thirds of the votes on that ballot then the Pope has not been elected; if however it turns out that someone has obtained two thirds of the votes, the canonically valid election of the Roman Pontiff has taken place.

- In the event that the Cardinal electors find it difficult to agree on the person to be elected, after balloting has been carried out for three days without result, voting is to be suspended for a maximum of one day in order to allow a pause for prayer and informal discussion among the voters.

- Voting is then resumed in the usual manner, and after seven ballots, if the election has not taken place, there is another pause for prayer, discussion and an exhortation. Nevertheless, there can be no waiving of the requirement that a valid election takes place only by an absolute majority of the votes or else by voting only on the two

The Sistine Chapel of the Apostolic Palace in the Vatican, prepared for the election of the Supreme Pontiff; in the foreground the stove for burning the ballots.

names which in the ballot immediately preceding have received the greatest number of votes; an absolute majority is required in the second case.

- When the election has canonically taken place, the junior Cardinal Deacon summons the Secretary of the College of Cardinals and the Master of Papal Liturgical Celebrations into the election hall. Then the Cardinal Dean, in the name of the whole College of electors, asks the consent of the one elected with the following words: *do you accept your canonical election as supreme pontiff ?* And, as soon as he has received the consent, he asks him: *by whath name do you wish to be called ?*

- Right after the senior Cardinal Deacon announces to the people waiting that the election has taken place and proclaims the name of the new Pope, who immediately thereafter imparts the Apostolic Blessing *Urbi et Orbi* from the balcony of the Vatican Basilica.

THE PORTRAITS OF THE POPES

Out of the many iconographies on the Supreme Pontiffs, from St. Peter to the present day, only three collections are considered to be complete.

The First, highly valued and officially acknowledged by the Vatican, is found in the naves of the Patriarchal Basilica of S. Paolo Fuori le Mura. The reproductions in this book are from this collection. The collection is made of medallions in mosaic, each one has the Pontiff's name written in Latin and the period of his pontificate in Roman numbers. This iconography was started by St. Leo the Great in 498 and historically updated in 1947.

The Second collection consists of oil paintings kept in the Altieri palace in Oriolo Romano (VT). They were commissioned in 1670 by Pope Clement X of the Altieri family. Along the side of each portrait there is a scroll upon which (up to Celestine II, 1143) there are brief notes about the Pontificate. After 1143, each scroll contains a written phrase from the prophecies of St. Malachi and the dates of election and death.

The Third complete collection is updated and found in the Basilica of Superga (TO). It was started after the Temple's consecration in 1731. The portraits, located in a large central room, are oval and square-shaped oil paintings on canvas. These are considered to be the first portraits to depict a true resemblance of their subjects since the time of Pope Martin V.

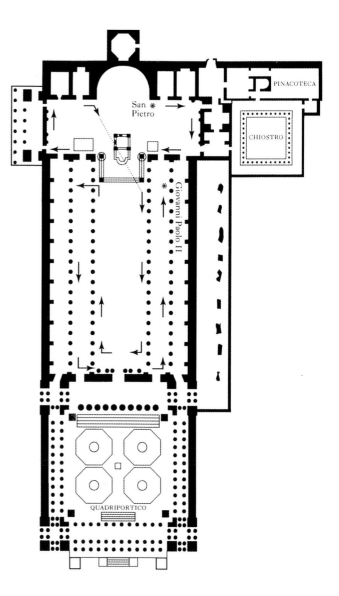

Floor plan of the Patriarchal Basilica of S. Paolo. The diagram indicates the sequence to be followed to view the Popes portraits reproduced in this volume.
The dots in the diagram represent the columns.

THE SUPREME ROMAN PONTIFFS

The inside of the Patriarchal Basilica of S. Paolo is divided into five naves. The reproductions of the Supreme Pontiffs printed in this volume were taken from the mosaic collection positioned above the arches: from St. Peter (on the right transept) to the present Pope along the central and the two lateral naves. (see diagram on page. 6).

PETER, ST.
42 - 67

LINUS, ST.
67 - 76

1 – Born in Bethsaida, Galilee - died June 29, 67. He received from Jesus the supreme pontifical power to be passed on to his successors.

It has been said that after having denied his association to Jesus, he cried for the rest of his life, leaving his cheeks furrowed by the tears. At the time of his arrival in Rome there were about sixty thousand Jews and nine synagogues. He instituted the first ecclesiastical code and the recitation of the "Our Father". He suffered martyrdom in Nero's time and when arrested he asked to be crucified head downwards. He was buried in a grave over which Constantine built the basilica that has become the present-day Basilica of St. Peter.

2 – Born in Volterra. Elected in 67 - died November 23, 76. He is buried beside St. Peter. He named the first 15 bishops and allowed women to enter churches and attend functions only if their heads were covered. The evangelists Mark and Luke were martyred during his pontificate. He was buried "iuxta corpus Beati Petri".

A tomb with the inscription "Linus" was discovered during an excavation in the area where the baldachin was to be erected. He pontificated for 11 years, 3 months and 12 days.

ANACLETUS, ST.
76 - 88

CLEMENT I, ST.
88 - 97

3 – Roman. Elected in 76, - died a martyr in 88. He established the rules for the consecration of the bishops, had a chapel built near St. Peter's tomb, for the burial of martyrs and instituted the rules for ecclesiastical dress. Anacletus divided the area of Rome in 25 parishes and appointed a deacon to each parish, creating the process of the "tituli". He was the first pontiff that used a salutation with apostolic blessing. He governed the Church for 12 years, during the reign of the emperors Vespasiano, Titus and Domitian. He is the patron of Ruvo (Puglia region) and was buried near the tomb of St. Peter.

4 – Roman. Elected in 88 - died a martyr in 97. The Emperor Trajan exiled him to Pontus and there he was thrown into the sea with an anchor tied around his neck. An anchor is represented on his tomb in memory of his martyrdom and he is the patron of Bruge's watermen. He reinstated the Sacrament of Confirmation according to the rites of St. Peter. The use of the word "amen" in religious ceremonies is attributed to his time as well as the "Dominus Vobiscum" said at the beginning of mass. He was buried on the site were the church bearing his name now stands. He sat on the St. Peter's chair for 9 years, 2 months and 10 days.

EVARISTUS, ST.
97 - 105

ALEXANDER I, ST.
105 - 115

5 – Greek. Elected in 97 - died in 105. Due to the intense growth of the Christian community he sub-divided the city into parishes. He instituted the first seven deaconster made of elderly priests who were later called Cardinals; this is believed to be the origin of the Sacred College. He decreed that weddings had to be blessed by a priest and introduced the Christians to keeping holy water in their houses. He is the author of the rite for church consecration.

He was buried near St. Peter after having been a pontiff for 9 years, 7 months and 2 days.

6 – Roman. Elected in 105 - died in 115. A disciple of Plutarch. He instituted the use of holy water in churches and houses and prescribed that the hosts to be consecrated were to be made with unleavened dough. He decreed that the wine for the Holy Sacrifice had to be diluted with water in memory of the chest wound inflicted on Jesus and decreed that priests could not celebrate more than one mass a day. He was buried in the church of S. Sabina. He governed the Church for 10 years, 7 months and 8 days.

SIXTUS I, ST.
115 - 125

TELESPHORUS, ST.
125 - 136

7 – Roman. Elected in 115 - died in 125. He ordered that the corporal be of linen, that holy furnishing be touched only by priests and he also established that the "Trisagio" be sung before mass. He was first buried near the tomb of St. Peter, but in 1132 Pope Innocent II granted him to the people of Alife who asked to have his remains. It is said that during the trip from Rome to Alife, the mule that was carrying the relics stopped in Alatri and would not go any further. The people of Alatri kept the relics in the town cathedral and the people of Alife received a finger bone of Sixtus1.

He governed for 9 years, 3 months and 21 days.

8 – Born in Greece. Elected in 125 - died a martyr in 136. He composed the chant "Gloria In Excelsis Deo" and instituted the seven-week fast and penance before Easter in memory of the fast and penance that Jesus went through while he was in the desert, this practice is still alive and is known as "Lent". He established that priests could celebrate three masses on Christmas Eve and he also introduced new prayers; subsequently, he is represented with a chalice and three hosts. He was buried near St. Peter' s tomb after having governed the Church for 11 years, 2 months and 21 days.

HYGINUS, ST.
136 - 140

PIUS I, ST.
140 - 155

9 – Born in Athens. Elected in 136 - died a martyr in 140. He determined the different prerogatives of the clergy and defined the grades of ecclesiastical hierarchy; appointed 6 bishops, 15 priests and 6 deacons. He instituted the role of godparents at the time of baptism for the purpose of guiding the child in his Christian life and ordered that churches should be dedicated. He was buried near the tomb of St. Peter. His pontificate was short : 4 years, 3 months and 4 days.

10 – Born in Aquileia. Elected in 140 - died a martyr in 155. The choice of the date for the celebration of Easter, as the first Sunday after the March full moon, is attributed to Pius I. He established new and important rules for the conversion of Jews to the Christian faith. He opposed the heresy of the Gnostic Marcion. His pontificate was during the reign of Antonius Pius: a relatively peaceful time. He had a small chapel built on the site where the church of St. Prassede stands today; the church was later commissioned by Pope Pascal I and preserves the column where Jesus was tide up and flagellated. Pius I was buried near St. Peter's tomb after a pontificate of about 15 years.

ANICETUS I, ST.
155 - 166

SOTER, ST.
166 - 175

11 – Born in Syria. Elected in 155 - died a martyr in 166. He decreed that the clergy could not have long hair. He confirmed that Easter be celebrated on Sunday according to St. Peter's tradition. He suffered martyrdom in 166, his body rests in the Chapel of the Altemps Palace in Rome. The urn containing his body was used as a sepulchre for Alexander Severius. Anicetus was Pope for about 11 years.

12 – Born in Fondi. Elected in 166 - died a martyr in 175. A generous and charitable Pope. The years of his pontificate coincided with the best years of the reign of emperor Marcus Aurelius. He forbade women to burn incense during a congregation of the faithful. He declared that any marriage which had not been blessed by a priest was not considered valid and established that priests were to celebrate mass on a empty stomach. His body rests in the Roman Church of S. Martino. He was a pontiff for a little over 9 years.

ELEUTHERIUS, ST.
175 - 189

VICTOR I, ST.
189 - 199

13 – Born at Nicopolis in Epirus. Elected in 175 - died a martyr in 189. King Lucius of England and his people were converted to Christianity, through baptism, by Fugazius and Damian who were sent by Eleutherius upon request of the king. He dispensed the Christians from following several dietary laws of Jewish origin. He is buried in the Vatican Grottoes . His pontificate lasted more than 14 years.

14 – Born in Africa. Martyr. Elected in 189, he died in 199. He established that any kind of water could be used for the celebration of baptism in a case of an emergency. He fought against the bishops of Asia and Africa to establish the celebration of Easter on Sunday, according to Roman rights and without any Jewish customs. He succeeded, with regard to the day, to establish Sunday as the celebration day and never to have it on the same day as the Hebrew Easter. During the third century, all the Christian churches adhered to these newly established days. The Ghirlandaio painted his portrait, dressed in his pontifical attire, in the Sistine Chapel. He was buried in the Vatican Grottoes after having pontificated for 10 years.

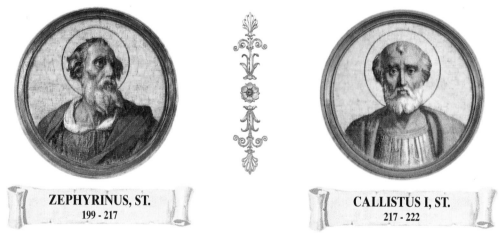

ZEPHYRINUS, ST.
199 - 217

CALLISTUS I, ST.
217 - 222

15 – Born in Rome. Elected in 199 - died a martyr in 217. He decreed that from the age of 14 everybody had to receive the Holy Communion on Easter Sunday. His pontificate was characterized by bitter theological struggles. He excommunicated Tertullian, introduced the use of the paten and forbade the use of the wooden chalice, replacing it with a glass chalice. Later on, the glass chalice was replaced with a chalice made of precious metals. At the beginning of the third century, the symbol of sanctity, "the halo", around the heads of angels, saints and the Blessed Virgin started to appear on every representation of these figures. His body rests in the Roman Church of San Silvestro in Capite. He was a pontiff for over 18 years.

16 – Born in Rome. Elected in 217 - died a martyr in 222. Callistus was the conceiver of the famous Catacombs on the Appian Way, where 46 popes and about 200,000 martyrs are buried. Imprisoned and exiled to Sardinia, by the Jews, he was condemned to work in the caves: he apparently forbade matrimony between relatives. He was beaten to death and thrown into a well where the Church of Santa Maria in Trastevere now stands. He was buried in the cemetery of Caledopius on the Aurelian Way. His pontificate lasted a little over 5 years.
Fra' Diamante painted his portrait in the Sistine Chapel.

URBAN I, ST.
222 - 230

PONTIAN, ST.
230 - 235

17 – Born in Rome. Elected in 222 - died in 230. He was a fervent evangelizer and is responsible for St. Cecily's conversion to Christianity. St. Cecily sang to God in her heart while music was playing on her wedding day and has since been regarded as the patron of musicians. She died a martyr in 230 and Urban I had a church built in Trastevere, on the site of her martyrdom, where here remains now rest. Urban I consented to the acquisition of properties in the name of the Church. He was decapitated after 8 years of pontificate. Today he rests in the Roman Church of S. Prassede.

18 – Born in Rome. Elected August 21st, 230 - died September 28, 235. He ordered that the psalms be sung in churches and prescribed the recitation of the "Confiteor Deo" to the dying and the use of the "Dominus vobiscum" salutation. He was deported to Sardinia and condemned to work in the mines. He is the first Pope to have renounced the papacy; he did this in order to allow Anterus to become the new pastor of the Church. He died of suffering in the small island of Tavolara. His remains rest in the Church of S. Prassede. He governed the church for 5 years, 2 months and 7 days.

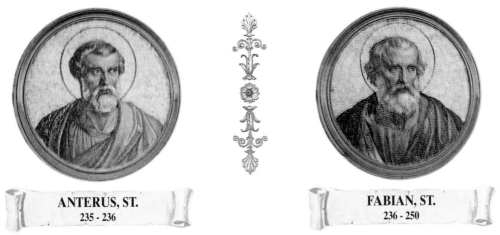

ANTERUS, ST.
235 - 236

FABIAN, ST.
236 - 250

19 – From Magna Grecia. Elected December 21st, 235. He suffered martyrdom under the Emperor Maximus, a barbarian from Thrace. He ordered that the acts and relics of the martyrs be collected and preserved in churches in a special place called the "Scrinium".
His pontificate lasted only 43 days. He was martyrized while Pontian was still alive in Sardinia. He is buried in the Roman Church of San Silvestro in Capite.

20 – Born in Rome. Elected January 10, 236 - died January 20, 250. During the election period, a dove settled on Fabian's head and this was interpreted as a positive sign from God and he was subsequently elected. During his pontificate Rome celebrated its first millennium with great solemnity and pagan feasts. The Christians suffered ferocious persecutions by Emperor Decius; many fled Rome to find refuge elsewhere and started the phenomenon of the anchorites.
Due to the persecutions even the church was left without a pope for 18 months but it was governed by the deacons. Fabian's pontificate lasted 14 years and 10 days. He is buried in the Roman Church of S. Prassede.

CORNELIUS, ST.
251 - 253

LUCIUS I, ST.
253 - 254

21 – Born in Rome. Elected March 251 - died June 253.
The first schism took place during his pontificate because of the election of the Anti-pope Novatian, who was later excommunicated during a Council held in Rome. He died in Civitavecchia were he had been exiled after refusing to offer sacrifices to the pagan gods, but he was not martyrized. At the time of Pope Cornelius the Church of Rome had 154 officers: 4 priests, 7 deacons, 7 junior deacons, 42 acolytes, 52 exorcists, readers and host givers. He is buried in the church of Santa Maria in Trastevere in Rome. His pontificate lasted 2 years and 3 months.

22 – Born in Rome. Elected June 25, 253 - died March 5, 254. A Pope of ascetic nature, he prohibited cohabitation between men and women not related by blood and decreed that clergies could not live with deaconesses even if given lodging for reasons of charity. It seems that he was elected in Civitavecchia were he had followed Cornelius in exile. Before dying, he entrusted his supreme pontifical powers to his Archdeacon Stephen and pledged for his election as successor. He is buried in the Church of S. Cecilia.

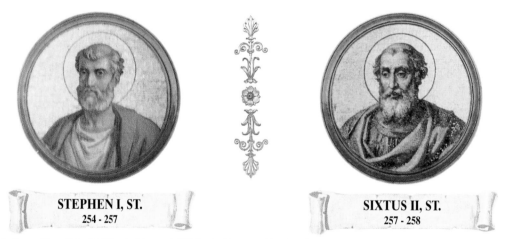

STEPHEN I, ST.
254 - 257

SIXTUS II, ST.
257 - 258

23 – Born in Rome. Elected May 12, 254 - died August 2, 257. During his pontificate, the struggle against the schismatic followers of Novatian flared up again. He used a ring with his name and a cross on it as a seal and started the origin of the piscatory ring. He prohibited the priests from wearing liturgical clothes outside of the church. Stephen was beheaded during a religious function in the catacombs of St. Callisto while seated on his episcopal chair. He is buried in the Church of San Silvestro in Capite. He was a pontiff for 3 years and 3 months.

24 – Born in Greece. Elected August 30, 257 - died a martyr August 6, 258. Of gentle disposition, he settled the disputes that had arisen under Cornelius, Lucius and Stephen. Because of another persecution of the Christians he feared for the mortal remains of St. Peter and St. Paul and hid them in a crypt along the Appian way called "ad Catacumbas", presently known as San Sebastiano. The exclamation "Deo Gratias" was pronounced for the first time during the martyrdom of St. Cyprian. He is buried in the Vatican Grottoes. His pontificate lasted less than one year.

DIONYSIUS, ST.
256 - 268

FELIX I, ST.
269 - 274

25 – Born in Turio. Elected July 22, 256 - died December 26, 268. He was elected a year after his predecessor because of the persecutions against the Christians. At the time, the barbarians were storming at the gates of the Roman empire. He reorganized the parishes of Rome and obtained liberty for the Christians imprisoned by Gallienus. A few months after his election, the emperor promoted new laws in favour of Christians and the Church was able to regain possession of many properties, such as buildings and cemeteries. He is the first Pope not to be a martyr. His body rests in the Roman Church of San Silvestro in Capite. He was a pontiff for 9 years and 6 months.

26 – Born in Rome. Elected January 5, 269 - died December 30, 274. He asserted the divinity and humanity of Jesus Christ and the doctrine of two natures in one person. He suffered the persecutions of Emperor Aurelian. He started the custom of burying martyrs under church altars, the celebration of mass on their tombs and liturgical regulations for the cult of martyrs in the catacombs: "hic constituit supra memorias martyrum missas celebrare". He is buried in the Roman Church of S. Prassede. He was a pontiff for almost 6 years.

EUTYCHIAN, ST.
275 - 283

CAIUS, ST.
283 - 296

27 – Born at Luni in Etruria. Elected January 4, 275 - died December 7, 283. He ordered that martyrs be wrapped with red Dalmatics: a rich tunic reserved for Roman emperors. These tunics are worn by deacons in solemn present-day functions . He insituted the blessing of the crops and ordered that drunkards be excommunicated until they regained control of this problem. His body has been transferred to the Cathedral of Sarzana. He was Pope for almost 9 years.

28 – Born at Salona, in Dalmatia. Elected December 17, 283 - died a martyr April 22, 296. He suffered martyrdom, not ordered by his uncle Diocletian. He established that a bishop could be nominated only if he had already been a hostarius, reader, acolyte, exorcist, subdeacon, deacon and a priest. He started, by accepting the adoration, the ritual of kissing the foot. With the transfer of the capital of the Empire from Rome to Nicomedia, Caius witnessed the beginning of the events that under Constantine established Rome as the exclusive site of the papacy. He is buried in the Roman Church of San Silvestro in Capite. He was a pontiff for a little over 12 years.

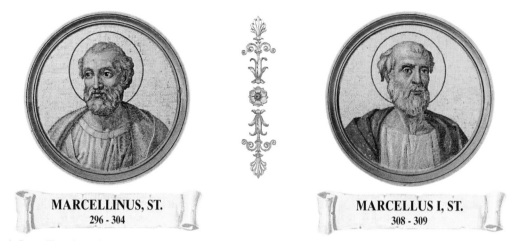

MARCELLINUS, ST.
296 - 304

MARCELLUS I, ST.
308 - 309

29 – Born in Rome. Elected June 30, 296 - died a martyr October 25, 304. During his period the persecutions of Diocletian reached their peak. Churches were destroyed and holy books burned. St. Lucy, St. Agnes, St. Bibiana, St. Sebastian and St. Lucian were among the many martyrs of that period. Marcellinus feared the profanation of the catacombs and filled them with earth to avoid this from happening. Before dying, he threatened to excommunicate whoever was going to bury his body and, for this reason, he remained above ground for about 40 days until St. Peter appeared to Marcellus and ordered him to bury the pontiff. Marcellinus is buried in the Roman Church of the SS. Apostoli. His pontificate lasted 8 years and 4 months.

30 – Born in Rome. Elected May 27, 308 - died a martyr January 16, 309. He was elected after four years of vacancy. He dealt with the difficult problem of pardoning those who had recanted for fear during the persecutions. He decreed that a council could not be held without the authorization of the Pope. He is the patron of grooms. Persecuted by Maxentius, he took refuge in the home of the matron Lucina and it is said that her house is the present-day Church of S. Marcello, the site where his body was buried. He was in charge of the Church for less than a year.

EUSEBIUS, ST.
309

MILTIADES, ST.
311 - 314

31 – Born in Cassano Ionico (of Greek origin). Elected April 18, 309 - died a martyr August 17, 309. St. Helen, mother of Constantine, recovered the Holy Cross in Jerusalem during his pontificate. He had to solve the question of pardoning the apostates, which was bringing the church to the point of a schism. He succeeded by maintaining a position of firmness and pardon. He ordered that the corporal be made of linen and consecrated by a bishop.
He suffered martyrdom in Sicily. His remains are in the Church of San Sebastiano Fuori le Mura. He was a pontiff for 121 days.

32 – Born in Africa. Elected July 2, 311 - died January 2, 314. He witnessed the triumph of Christianity. With the edict of tolerance for the Christian faith, issued by Emperor Constantine, and after the vision "in hoc signo vinces" this faith became the state religion. The blessing of the bread started around this time.
He had the Basilica of San Giovanni in Laterano built and convoked the first council that was headed by a Pope and sanctioned by the Empire. He was the last pontiff to be buried in the catacombs of San Callisto. Today he rests in the Roman Church of San Silvestro in Capite. He was Pope for about 2 and a half years.

SILVESTER I, ST.
314 - 335

MARK, ST.
336

33 – Born in Rome. Elected January 31, 314 - died December 31, 335. He celebrated the first Ecumenical Council at Nicea and it was at this time that the "Credo" was composed. Silvester was the first to use a lead seal during the solemn acts: the seal had his name and the apostles' heads imprinted on it. He instituted Sunday as a holiday dedicated to God in memory of the creation and was the first Pope to wear the tiara. He created the "Iron Crown" with a nail from the Holy Cross. The Church of S. Giovanni in Laterano became Rome's cathedral and was consecrated by Silvester on November 9, 324. Emperor Constantine the Great, who was baptized by Silvester, started planning the St. Peter's Basilica in the Vatican. Silvester was buried in the Roman Church of S. Silvestro in Capite. His pontificate lasted almost 22 years.

34 – Born in Rome. Elected January 18, 336 - died October 7, 336. He decreed that the Pope should be consecrated by the Bishop of Ostia. He instituted the "Pallium" which is still in use today: a white wool long scarf, made from two blessed white lambs and decorated with black crosses. His Pallium is preserved in a silver casket near St. Peter's tomb. During his pontificate, the first religious calendar was drawn up. He had two churches built: the Santa Balbina on the Appian way and San Marco at Piazza Venezia. Mark was buried in the Roman Church that bears his name. He was a Pope for less than a year.

JULIUS I, ST.
337 - 352

LIBERIUS
352 - 366

35 – Born in Rome. Elected February 6, 337 - died April 12, 352. He ordered the Eastern church to celebrate Christmas on the 25th of December instead of January 6th, the Epiphany. He is considered to be the founder of the archives of the Holy See. The oldest portrayal of a Pope on his papal chair is the one of Julius I seated on an extraordinarily ornate chair in a blessing pose. His body is buried in the Church of Santa Maria in Trastevere in Rome. He was a pontiff for 15 years.

36 – Born in Rome. Elected May 17, 352 - died November 24, 366. The polemics with the Arians continued and lead to the election of the anti-pope Felix II. Liberius started the work for the foundation of the Basilica of Santa Maria Maggiore on a perimeter that he traced after a snowfall on August 15. He ordered that disputes were not to be settled and payments were to be postponed on days of fasting. He is the first Pope without the title of Saint. He was exiled to France because of disagreements with the Emperor Constance. He is buried in the Vatican Grottoes. His pontificate lasted a little over 14 years.

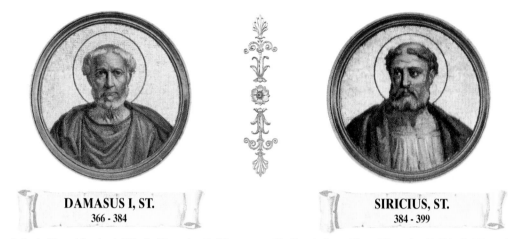

DAMASUS I, ST.
366 - 384

SIRICIUS, ST.
384 - 399

37 – Born in Spain. Elected October 1, 366 - died December 11, 384. Damasus was a learned Pope. He authorized the signing of the psalms by alternate choirs (Ambrosian rite) instituted by St. Ambrogio. He commissioned the translation of the Sacred Scripture,
introduced the use of the word "Alleluia", and called the 2nd Ecumenical Council. He is especially remembered for the restoration of the catacombs and the construction and care of churches and monuments. He is buried in the Church of San Lorenzo in Damaso in Rome that was built during his pontificate. His pontificate lasted 18 years.

38 – Born in Rome. Elected December 15, 384 - died November 26, 399. He was the first, from the time of St. Peter, to assume the title of Pope, from the Greek "papa" which means father although others believe it is a anagram formed from "Petri, Apostoli, Potestatem, Accipiens". He sustained the necessity of celibacy for priests and deacons. During his pontificates many churches were built, including the Basilica of San Paolo in the same proportion as it is today. He is buried in the Church of S. Prassede in Rome. He governed the Church for about 15 years.

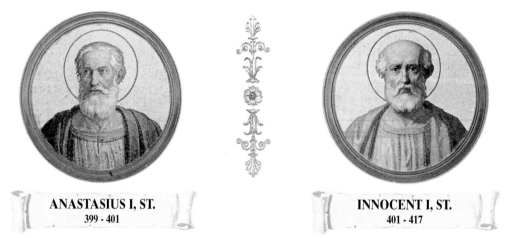

ANASTASIUS I, ST.
399 - 401

INNOCENT I, ST.
401 - 417

39 – Born in Rome. Elected November 27, 399 - died December 19, 401. He settled the schism between Rome and the Church of Antiochia. He vigorously fought the followers of immoral practices who maintained that the divinity was also hidden in material things. He prescribed that priests must stand while listening to the Gospels and that no one with physical defects could become a priest. His remains rest in the Church of San Martino ai Monti in Rome. He was Pope for a little over 2 years.

40 – Born in Albano (Rome). Elected December 22, 401 - died March 12, 417. He witnessed the sacking of Rome by the Goths of Alaric. He established the observance of the Roman rites, the catalogue of canonical books. He ruled the relations between the Christians, the Jews and the pagans. He persuaded Honorius to prohibit gladiator contests in the circus. Innocent I confirmed the tradition of not celebrating mass on Holy Friday. He is buried in the Church of San Martino ai Monti in Rome. He governed the Church for 15 years and 3 months.

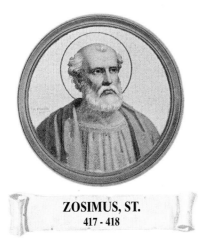

ZOSIMUS, ST.
417 - 418

BONIFACE I, ST.
418 - 422

41 – Of Greek origin (Masuraca). Elected March 18, 417- died December 26, 418. He had a strong personality, claimed the right of the church against foreign interferences. He sent vicars to the Gauls.
Of very high moral standards, he ruled that illegitimate children and slaves could not become clerics and prohibited priests to go into taverns to drink wine. His body is conserved in the Basilica of San Lorenzo Fuori le Mura. His pontificate lasted about a year and a half.

42 – Born in Rome. Elected December 28, 418 - died November 4, 422. The interference of Charles of Ravenna marks the beginning of the interferences in the elections of the Pope. Boniface I was confirmed Pope after several months of opposition by another contender: the anti-pope Eulalius. He ruled that nobody could become a priest before the age of thirty and anyone with debts could become a cleric. He was buried in the Vatican Grottoes. He governed the Church for almost 4 years.

CELESTINE I, ST.
422 - 432

SIXTUS III, ST.
432 - 440

43 – Born in Rome. Elected November 10, 422 - died July 27, 432. He called the third Ecumenical Council which condemned Nestorius, Patriarch of Constantinople. During this council it was proclaimed that the Bishop of Rome had supremacy over all the churches.
He sent St. Patrick on a mission to Ireland. The use of the "pastoral staff" starts to be mentioned during his time. His body is buried in the Church of Santa Prassede in Rome. His pontificate lasted about 10 years.

44 – Born in Rome. Elected July 31, 432- died August 19, 440. He enlarged and embellished the Basilicas of Santa Maria Maggiore and San Lorenzo. In 440, he started the construction of another church dedicated to Lorenzo: the existing San Lorenzo in Lucina. Sixtus III was the author of many epistles and he upheld the jurisdiction of Rome, over the Illyria, against the eastern emperor who wanted it to be dependent on Constantinople. His body is buried in the Basilica of San Lorenzo Fuori le Mura. He was a pontiff for a little over a year.

LEO I, ST.
440 - 461

HILARUS, ST.
461 - 468

45 – Born in the Tuscia region. Elected November 29 - died September 10, 461. Leo was called the "Great" for his energetic and able work in maintaining the unity of the church. He called the 4th Ecumenical Council and defined the mystery of the incarnation. He went to confront Attila, King of the Huns, and induced him to withdraw from coming to Rome. He was buried in the old Constantinian Basilica on the site which is today called "Cappella della Colonna". His pontificate lasted 21 years.

46 – Born in Cagliari. Elected November 19, 461 - died February 29, 468. With his political matters he followed the school of his great predecessor. He established that a certain level of culture was necessary to become a priest and decided that neither a Pope nor the bishops could nominate their successors. He instituted an Apostolic Vicariate in Spain and founded two libraries at the Basilica of San Giovanni in Laterano. The libraries were later rearranged by Nicholas V and then transferred to the Vatican; they became the first nucleus of the Vatican Library. He is buried in the Roman Basilica of San Lorenzo Fuori le Mura. He governed for almost 7 years.

SIMPLICIUS, ST.
468 - 483

FELIX III, ST.
483 - 492

47 – Born in Tivoli. Elected March 3, 468 - died March 10, 483. During his pontificate the Western Empire came to an end and the schism led to the founding of the churches of Armenia, Syria and Egypt (Copts). He regulated the distribution of offerings to the pilgrims and new churches. He was the first Pope that addressed an emperor using the formula "Dear son". He subdivided Rome into five districts, the same number as that of the Roman Basilicas. He is buried in the St. Peter's Basilica. He was a pontiff for 15 years.

48 – Born in Rome. Elected March 13, 483 - died March 1st, 492. He tried to restore peace in the turmoiled Eastern Church. Before being elected he had sons, one of them was the father of the famous St. Gregory the Great. He wished to be buried in the Basilica of San Paolo Fuori le Mura, where his family tomb was located. He is the only Pope buried in this Basilica. His pontificate lasted 9 years.

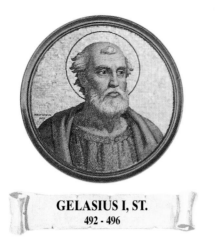

GELASIUS I, ST.
492 - 496

ANASTASIUS II
496 - 498

49 – Born in Rome and of African origins. Elected March 1st, 492 - died November 21, 496. He instituted the Code for the uniforming of rites and ceremonies. Due to his charitable generosity toward the needy, he was called "Father of the poor people". He maintained the supremacy of the Church over that of the Kings. He introduced into the mass, the Greek invocation "Kyrie Eleison" "God have mercy" and instituted the feast of the Purification (Ash day). The invocation for the dead "Requiem Aeternam" used in the Latin rites comes from the IV book of Esra. At this time, the mitre becomes an essential piece for the priest to use during religious ceremonies. He is buried in the Vatican Grottoes. He governed 4 years and 8 months.

50 – Born in Rome. Elected November 24, 496 - died November 19, 498. During his pontificate Clovis, King of the Franks, was converted to Christianity and Anastasius baptized him together with 3000 other Franks. In his own way, he was so irresolute about putting an end to the schism to the point that he was accused of heresy; Dante placed him in hell because of this reputation. He is buried in the Vatican Grottoes. His pontificate lasted 2 years.

SYMMACHUS, ST.
498 - 514

HORMISDAS, ST.
514 - 523

51 – Born in Sardinia. Elected November 22, 498 - died July 19, 514. He legitimated the ecclesiastical properties and assigned them to the clergy for their use. He redeemed all the slaves and gave them their freedom. The construction of the first Vatican Palace is attributed to him as well as the fountains in St. Peter's Square. During a synod in 499, he ordered that the election process for a new Pope could not take place if the governing Pope was still alive. He is buried in the Vatican Grottoes. He was a pontiff for 15 years and 8 months.

52 – Born in Frosinone. Elected July 20, 514 - died August 6, 523. During his pontificate St. Benedict founded his order and the famous abbey in Montecassino, which was completely destroyed by the bombing of 1944. He established that bishops could not be ordained in exchange for privileges. He is buried in the Vatican Grottoes. He was a Pope for about 9 years.

JOHN I, ST.
523 - 526

FELIX IV, ST.
526 - 530

53 – Born in Populonia. Elected August 13, 523 - died a martyr May 8, 526. He was the first Pope that went to Constantinople and the first that solemnly crowned an emperor. He was imprisoned by the barbaric King Theodoric and placed in a jail in Ravenna, where he died. He is buried in the Vatican Grottoes. His pontificate lasted 2 years and 9 months.

54 – Born in Benevento. Elected July 12, 526 - died September 22, 530. Arbitrarily nominated Pope by King Theodoric for his own purposes, he showed such a loyalty towards the interests of the church that the king rejected him and had him outlawed. The Christians had the liberty to practice their religion restored after the king's death. Felix converted two pagan buildings, located in the Roman forum, into the church of Santi Cosma e Damiano. The two buildings were a gift from Amalasuntha, Queen of the Goths. He is buried in the Vatican Grottoes. He was a pontiff for 4 years and 4 months.

BONIFACE II
530 - 532

JOHN II
533 - 535

55 – Born in Rome. Elected November 22, 530 - died October 17, 532. Because of gothic origins he was considered "barbarous and foreigner": as a result the opposing anti-pope Dioscorus was elected. The ensuing struggle between the two Popes ended at the death of Dioscorus. Boniface had the monastery of Montecassino built on the temple of Apollo. He was the first Pope of German descent. He is buried in the Vatican Grottoes. He was a pontiff for about 2 years.

56 – Born in Rome. Elected January 2, 533 - died May 8, 535. He was the first Pope that changed his given name, since his name was that of a pagan god, Mercurius. That tradition was followed by all his successors with the exception of Hadrian VI. King Athalaric approved the decree, promulgated by the Roman senate, against simony and with an edict he confirmed the Pope as the chief of all bishops. He is buried in the Vatican Grottoes. His pontificate lasted 2 years and 4 months.

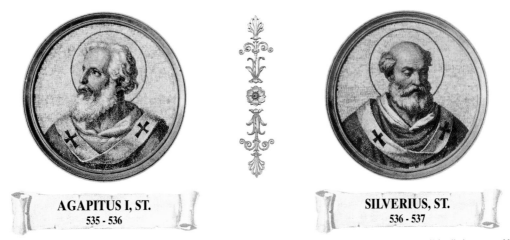

AGAPITUS I, ST.
535 - 536

SILVERIUS, ST.
536 - 537

57 – Born in Rome. Elected May 13, 535 - died April 22, 536. He was sent to Constantinople by the King of the Goths to intervene against the intentions of the Emperor Justinian to take back the control of Italy. He died there, poisoned by the Emperor's wife, Theodora, who was a follower of the Eutichian cult. The famous Cassiodoro started, on the Pope's request, the school for Christian science studies. He is buried in the Vatican Grottoes. He governed for about 11 months.

58 – Born in Frosinone. Elected June 1, 536 - died a martyr November 11, 537. Silverius met Belisario at Villa Pinciana where he was deposed, dressed as a simple monk and exiled to Lycia. Later when the Byzantine Army captured Rome, Silverius was ordered to renounce the papacy and exiled to the Island of Ponza where he was assassinated and buried. His pontificate lasted 1 year and 5 months.

VIGILIUS
537 - 555

PELAGIUS I
556 - 561

59 – Born in Rome, Elected March 22, 537 - died June 7, 555. Despite Theodora's efforts, he refused to revoke the condemnation of the Eutichian theories. He was arrested while celebrating mass but he managed to escape. He called the Fifth Ecumenical Council. During his pontificate, Justinian imposed the "pragmatic sanction" which limited papal judicial authority on religious matters. He died in Syracuse. His body was transferred to Rome and buried first in Priscilla's Cemetery but was later moved to the Vatican Grottoes. He was Pope for just over 18 years.

60 – Born in Rome. Elected April 16, 556 - died March 4, 561. His elevation to the papacy was influenced by Justinian, since Rome was now a province of the Byzantine Empire, but he remained faithful to the principles of catholic orthodoxy. He had the Church of the SS. Apostoli built in Rome. He is buried in the Vatican Grottoes. He governed the Church for 5 years.

JOHN III
561 - 574

BENEDICT I
575 - 579

61 – Born in Rome. Elected July 17, 561 - died July 13, 574. During his pontificate, Italy was invaded by the Longobards. John III helped the Italian people during the disastrous barbarian invasion, headed by Narses, in defence of their land and against the cruelties of the invaders. He saw to the completion of the SS. Apostoli Church and consecrated it on the day of the St. Philip and St. James. He is buried in the Vatican Grottoes. His pontificate lasted 13 years.

62 – Born in Rome. Elected June 2, 575 - died July 30, 579. He was elected after almost a year of vacancy of the See. He tried in vain to restore order in Italy and France, which were both devastated by barbaric invasions and internal disorders. He confirmed the Fifth Council of Constantinople. He is buried in the Vatican Grottoes. He was a Pope for 4 years and 1 month.

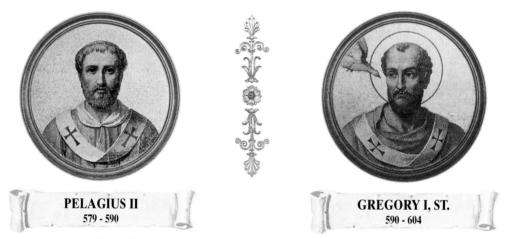

PELAGIUS II
579 - 590

GREGORY I, ST.
590 - 604

63 – Born in Rome and of Gothic descent. Elected November 26, 579 - died February 7, 590. He was elected without the Emperor's approval. It was the first step for the Holy See in detaching itself from Imperial authority, as deliberated by Justinian. He decreed that priests must recite the Divine Office every day and he started putting the date of indiction on documents. He died victim of a terrible plague which left victims to die yawning and sneezing. He is buried in the Vatican Grottoes. He was a pontiff for almost 11 years.

64 – Born in Rome. Elected September 3, 590 - died March 3, 604. He reaffirmed the civil authority of the Pope: the beginning of Temporal Powers. At the time of the plague, an angel appeared to him on the castle that has since been called Castel Sant'Angelo. He created a young choir for the purpose of embellishing the church ceremonies with chants. These were called "Gregorian chants", after his name, and they are still sung today during solemn functions. Gregory the Great was a devote and humble Pope. He liked to call himself "the servant of the servants of God". He is buried in the Clementine Chapel in the St. Peter's Basilica. His pontificate lasted 13 years and 5 months.

SABINIAN
604 - 606

BONIFACE III
607

65 – Born in Blera. Elected September 13, 604 - died February 22, 606. Before his election the Holy See remained vacant for 6 months. He regulated the ringing of the bells to remind people of the canonical hours for meditation and prayer. He ordered that oil lamps in the church must burn continuously. He always used a portable bell during functions. He is buried in the Vatican Grottoes. He was a Pope for 1 year and 5 months.

66 – Born in Rome. Elected February 19, 607 - died November 12, 607. He prohibited arrangements for the election of the new Pope until three days after the death of the reigning Pope. Later, Gregory X imposed a period of 9 days and Pius XI brought it up to 15 days to allow cardinals from far away countries to travel to Rome in time for the conclave. Boniface III established that only the Bishop of Rome could call himself Ecumenical. He is buried in Vatican Grottoes. He was pope for only 8 months and 23 days.

BONIFACE IV, ST.
608 - 615

ADEODATUS I, ST.
615 - 618

67 – Born in the Abruzzo region. Elected August 25, 608 - died May 8, 615.
He converted the Pantheon from a pagan temple, dedicated by Agrippa to all the gods, into a church dedicated to the Blessed Virgin and the Saints. He instituted All Saints Day on November 1st. The institution of a commemoration day for all the Christian dead is attributed to him. He morally and materially improved the lower clergy. His body rests in the Vatican Basilica. He governed the Church for 6 years and 8 months.

68 – Born in Rome. Elected October 10, 615 - died November 8, 618. He tended to the lepers and the plague-stricken with heroic deeds. His lead seal for official documents is known as the oldest and it is kept in the Vatican together with his first Papal Bull. He is buried in the Vatican Grottoes. His pontificate lasted 3 years and 19 days.

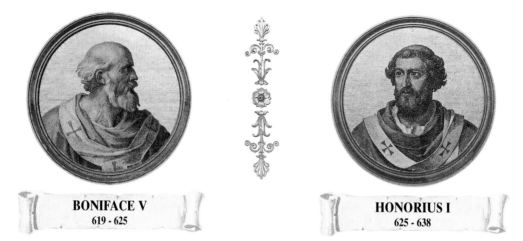

BONIFACE V
619 - 625

HONORIUS I
625 - 638

69 – Born in Naples. Elected December 23, 619 - died October 25, 625. The period of his pontificate began 11 months later and was embittered by the wars for the Crown of Italy. He established the immunity of asylum for those who were prosecuted and looked for shelter in churches. During his pontificate, Mohammed started his preachership. He is buried in the Vatican Grottoes. His pontificate lasted 5 years and 10 months.

70 – Born in Capua. Elected October 27, 625 - died October 12, 638. He sent missionaries almost all over the world. He introduced the feast of the Glorification of the Holy Cross which is celebrated on September 14. He solved the Eastern Church question and the Aquileia Schism for the three chapters of the 4th Chalcedon Council, which condemned Eutiche's heresy and was more than once confirmed and cancelled. He is buried in the Vatican Grottoes. His pontificate lasted almost 13 years.

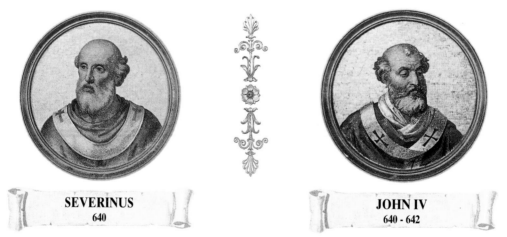

SEVERINUS
640

JOHN IV
640 - 642

71 – Born in Rome. Elected May 28, 640 - died August 2, 640. He was in serious disagreement with the Byzantine Emperor, Heraclius, since he condemned Monothelitism; in order to punish him, the King ordered to sack St. John's Church and the Lateran Palace. He died of grief. He is buried in the Vatican Grottoes. His pontificate lasted only 2 months and 5 days.

72 – Born in Dalmatia. Elected December 24, 640 - died October 12, 642. He tried to show the path of truth to the dissenters of Egypt. He transferred the mortal remains of the martyrs Venantius, Anastasius and Maurus to the Lateran. He personally ordained 28 priests and 18 bishops in order to be sure of their faith. He called back the Bishops from Scotland to celebrate Easter. He is buried in the Vatican Grottoes. His pontificate lasted 1 year, 9 months and 18 days.

THEODORE I
642 - 649

MARTIN I, ST.
649 - 655

73 – Born in Jerusalem. Elected November 24, 642 - died May 14, 649. He added the name Sovereign to the word Pope and gave a new order to the internal jurisdiction of the clergy. He was in serious disagreement with the Eastern Empire and its Emperor Constans the II and he supposedly died from poisoning. He concentrated on the collection of relics and we must be grateful to him for those of the Crib located in Santa Maria Maggiore. He is buried in the Vatican Grottoes. His pontificate lasted 6 years and 6 months.

74 – Born in Todi. Elected July 5, 649 - died September 16, 655.
He condemned Eastern Bishops, who were protected by the Byzantine Emperor. He was imprisoned and exiled and died in poverty on Cherso Island. He introduced the feast of the Immaculate Conception, celebrated on March 25. People say that Martin I was the first Pope who was already a bishop at the moment of the election. He is buried in the Roman Church of St. Martino ai Monti. The Church considers him a martyr. It is worth mentioning that his successor was elected one year before his death, since he was exiled by the Emperor Constans II; Martin did not object. His pontificate lasted 6 years and 2 months (or 4 years, if one considers the anticipated election of Eugene I).

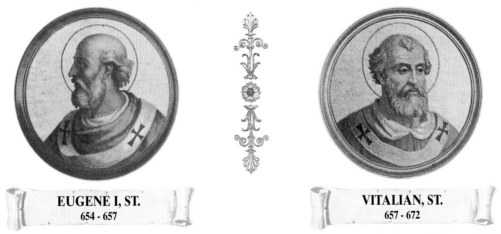

EUGENE I, ST.
654 - 657

VITALIAN, ST.
657 - 672

75 – Born in Rome. Elected August 10, 654 - died June 2, 657. He was elected one year before the death of Martin I. He opposed the intrigues of the Emperor by informing the European countries about the sad end of his predecessor. He introduced the vow of chastity for priests. He his buried in the Vatican Grottoes. His pontificate lasted 2 years and 10 months.

76 – Born in Segni. Elected July 30, 657 - died January 27, 672.
He sent Nuncios to Gaul, Spain and England. He was the first Pope to introduce the liturgical sound of the organ, allowing it to be used during religious rites. In 671 the Longobards were converted to Christianity. The separation between the catechumen and the secret part of the Faithful was eliminated by the Holy Mass. He is buried in the Vatican Grottoes. His pontificate lasted 14 years and 6 months.

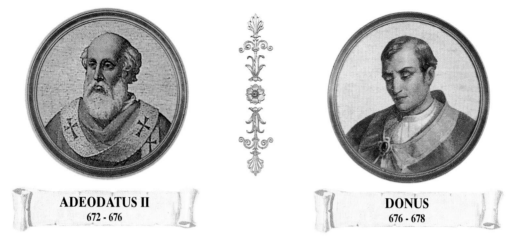

ADEODATUS II
672 - 676

DONUS
676 - 678

77 – Born in Rome. Elected April 11, 672 - died July 17, 676. With the help of his Missionaries, he succeeded in converting the Maronites, a strong people with an Armenian-Syrian origin. He was the first to pronounce the words "Greetings and Apostolic Blessing" during the lectures. He was the first Pope to sign his letters and acts during the years of his pontificate. He is buried in the Vatican Grottoes. His pontificate lasted 2 years and 6 months.

78 – Born in Rome. Elected November 2, 676 - died April 2, 678. During his pontificate, he put an end to the Schism of the Ravenna Church. He encouraged the bishops to foster the diffusion of the schools in Trier, in the Germanic Gaul and in Cambridge in England. He ordered that the atrium of the St. Peter Basilica, which was later given the name Heaven, be sumptuously paved with different marbles. He is buried in the Vatican Grottoes. His pontificate lasted 1 year and 5 months.

AGATHO, ST.
678 - 681

LEO II, ST.
682 - 683

79 – Born in Palermo. Elected June 27, 678 - died January 10, 681. He kept in touch with English bishops and fostered the development of Ireland into a cultural centre. He called the Sixth Ecumenical Council. He was defined a Thaumaturg, given his numerous miracles. Contrary to the habit of his predecessors, Agatho looked after the safe of the Roman Church personally. According to an improbable tradition, Agatho was supposedly 103 years old at the moment of his election; he apparently died four years later, rather than two, when he was 107. He is buried in the Vatican Grottoes. His pontificate lasted 2 years and 6 months.

80 – Born in Sicily. Elected August 17, 682 - died July 3, 683. He sumptuously celebrated religious services in order to make the faithful ever more aware of the majesty of the Lord and introduced the aspersion of holy water on the faithful during Christian rites. Since he was very keen to music, he could reform the singing of the liturgy and the concert of sacred hymns. He introduced the kiss of peace to the Mass. He is buried in St. Peter's Church in the Cappella della Colonna. His pontificate lasted only 10 months and a half.

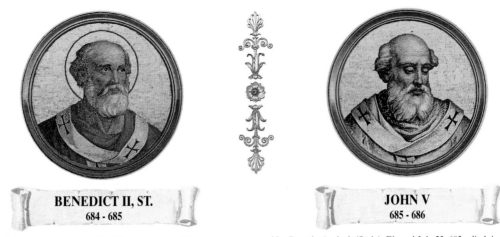

BENEDICT II, ST.
684 - 685

JOHN V
685 - 686

81 – Born in Rome. Elected June 26, 684 - died May 8, 685.
He reintroduced the immunity of asylum that opposing factions did not respect because they continued to arrest or kill their enemies, even in church. He managed to free the Church from the influence of the Emperor, dating back to Justinian, by eliminating the clause of Imperial consent. During his Pontificate, between Christmas and the Epiphany, an extremely bright comet appeared in the sky. He is buried in the Vatican Grottoes. His pontificate lasted about 1 year.

82 – Born in Antioch (Syria). Elected July 23, 685 - died August 2, 686. He was elected Pope in St. John Lateran's Church and was the first Pope to be consecrated without waiting for the abusive confirmation of the Imperial Court of Constantinople. He restored order in the Sardinian and Corsican dioceses by claiming the exclusive right of the Holy See to consecrate the bishops of the isles. He is buried in the Vatican Grottoes. His pontificate lasted about 1 year.

CONON
686 - 687

SERGIUS I, ST.
687 - 701

83 – Born in Thrace. Elected October 21, 686 - died September 21, 687. His pontificate was very restless given the serious anarchy that affected the Church. Platina says that Conon was defined Angelic because of his venerable grey hair and his dignified posture. He had to accept the reintroduction of the Imperial confirmation for the election of a new pope, which was imposed by the exarch from Ravenna. He was often the victim of cunning followers of the Byzantine Emperor. He supposedly died of poisoning. He is buried in the Vatican Grottoes. His pontificate lasted 11 months.

84 – Born in Antioch. Elected December 15, 687 - died September 8, 701. He was appointed after two anti-popes. He tried to repair the schism arisen in Rome and put an end to the Aquileia schism. He introduced the triple prayer of the Agnus Dei into the liturgy, which follows the break of the Host. During his pontificate, the Republic of Venice was established. He is buried in the Vatican Grottoes. His pontificate lasted almost 14 years.

JOHN VI
701 - 705

JOHN VII
705 - 707

85 – Born in Ephesus. Elected October 30, 701 - died January 11, 705. During particularly difficult moments for Christianity, whereby it was rejected in the East and in Spain by the Saracen Turks and started to spread all over Europe causing serious damage to Christian people, he defended the prerogatives of the Church against the Eastern Emperor and delivered many slaves. He is buried in the Vatican Grottoes. His pontificate lasted about 3 years.

86 – Born in Rossano di Calabria. Elected March 1, 705 - died October 18, 707. He did not give his consensus to the shady pretensions of the Emperor Justinian II, who gave way to the slaughters that had forced Latin and Italian peoples to abandon the Eastern Empire. We owe to John VII the golden mosaic (705) of the Epiphany, a work which was kept in the oratory of the old Basilica of St. Peter and can be currently found in the sacristy of Santa Maria in Cosmedin. He is buried in the Vatican Grottoes. His pontificate lasted 2 years and 8 months.

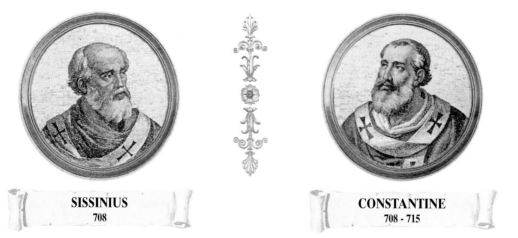

SISSINIUS
708

CONSTANTINE
708 - 715

87 – Born in Syria. Elected January 15, 708 - died February 4, 708. Given the short period of his pontificate, he did not leave significant works. He ordered the restoration of the Roman walls that had been damaged during the attacks and the continuing threats coming from the Longobards and Saracens. He is buried in the Vatican Grottoes.. He died after only 20 days of pontificate.

88 – Born in Syria. Elected March 25, 708 - died April 9, 715. He was forced to go to Byzantium where he restored peace between the Church and the Empire. He encouraged the Christians from Spain to react against the unfaithful. As a sign of obedience and worship, he introduced the kissing of the holy foot of the bronze statue of the Apostle Peter. He is buried in the Vatican Grottoes. His pontificate lasted about 7 years.

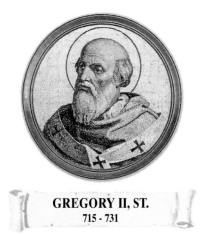

GREGORY II, ST.
715 - 731

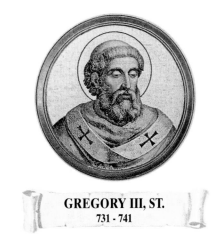

GREGORY III, ST.
731 - 741

89 – Born in Rome. Elected May 5, 715 - died February 11, 731.
As a response to the Constantinople edict, which forbade the worship of sacred images and ordered their destruction, the Italian provinces rose up against the army of Leo III that was marching towards Rome; the sect of the iconoclasts was defeated. He was the first Pope to mint coins: he had keys imprinted on them, which symbolize the Roman Church, and not his image, since he was very humble. He gave way to the pontifical mint. He made the monastic discipline flourish again all over Italy and excommunicated all those who had married a nun. Thanks to the donations from Liudprand, the first nucleus of the Pontifical State was created, which was then called Roman Duchy. He is buried in the Vatican Grottoes. His pontificate lasted 15 years and 9 months.

90 – Born in Syria. Elected March 18, 731 - died November 28, 741. He asked Charles Martel, King of Franks, for help against the Longobards: that is why he was afterwards called the "Most Christian", a name which was subsequently adopted by all French Kings. The charitable donations were defined "Peter's pence". During the Pontificate of Gregory III, the residence of the Pope was called "Sacred Palace". He is buried in the Vatican Grottoes. His pontificate lasted 10 years and 8 months.

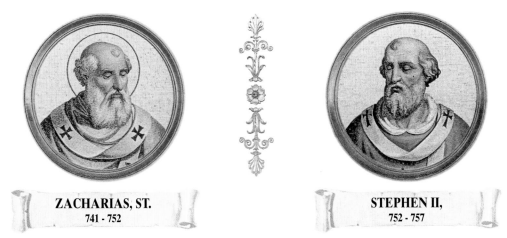

ZACHARIAS, ST.
741 - 752

STEPHEN II,
752 - 757

91 – Born in Calabria. Elected December 10, 741 - died March 22, 752. He firmly opposed Rachis, Earl of Friuli, from conquering Italy, Rachis later became a monk. He consecrated Pippin the Short as King of the Franks. This was the first appointment of a king made by a Pope. He ordered that the priests could not say Mass with a hat on and that churchmen should always wear a long habit, commonly called cassock. In the cathedral of Siena, the bust of the She-Pope Johanna was replaced with that of St. Zacharias. He is buried in the Vatican Grottoes. His pontificate lasted 10 years and 3 months.

92 – There were two Stephen II: the first lasted just one day (March 3); the second was elected on March 26, 757 and died on May 26, 757. His election gave rise to great enthusiasm and he was actually borne in triumph, starting the tradition of the gestatorial chair. In Canino (Viterbo) there is a bell dating back to this period, which was probably donated by Stephen. He was the first Pope to cross the Alps, when traveling to Pippin the Short to ask for protection from King Astolph. Furthermore, he was the first to be preceded by the Eucharist during his long journey. He is buried in the Vatican Grottoes. His pontificate lasted exactly 5 years and 1 month.

PAUL I, ST.
757 - 767

STEPHEN III
768 - 772

93 – Born in Rome. Elected May 29, 757 - died June 28, 767. He fostered a close relationship with the Greek Church. He visited jails redeeming prisoners who had been condemned because of debts. He discovered the remains of St. Petronilla, who according to tradition was St. Peter's daughter. He founded, in the paternal home, the monastery and the church of S. Silvestro in Capite. He was the godfather of Pippin's daughter, who co-operated closely with him with the aim of introducing the Roman chant in his kingdom. He is buried in the Vatican Grottoes. His pontificate lasted about 10 years.

94 – Born in Sicily. Elected August 7, 768 - died January 24, 772. He was preceded by two anti-popes. He showed the straight and narrow path to Charlemagne, King of the Franks, and helped the Christians in Palestine in every possible way. During the Lateran Council, organized by Stephen III, it was decided that lay people could not become popes and the right to participate in the election of the Pope was abolished, limiting their participation to the simple acclamation of the person chosen by the clergy. He is buried in the Vatican Grottoes. His pontificate lasted 3 years and 5 months.

HADRIAN I
772 - 795

LEO III, ST.
795 - 816

95 – Born in Rome. Elected February 9, 772 - died December 25, 795. He restored the Roman walls and the old aqueducts. We owe to him the golden statue of St. Peter's sepulchre and the silver pavement in front of the altar of the confession. He called the 7th Ecumenical Council. He is buried in Vatican City. The pontificate of Hadrian was one of the longest, after St. Peter's, lasting 23 years, 10 months and 17 days: the 25 years of Pius VI (1775-1800), the 32 of Pius IX (1846-1878) and the 25 of Leo XIII (1878-1903) were still to come.

96 – Born in Rome. Elected December 27, 795 - died June 12, 816. He was the first Pope to have been crowned with a tiara of white cloth like a helmet. With the crowning of Charlemagne, which took place in the Basilica of St. Peter on Christmas night of the year 800, the Western Empire was restored and called the Holy Roman Empire. This was the first imperial crowning made by a Pope in Rome. In the Basilica of San Giovanni in Laterano he ordered the painting of numerous windows decorated with stained glass. He was the first to have the words "Dominus Noster" imprinted on coins. He founded the Palatine School, which gave origin to the University of Paris. He is buried in the Basilica of St. Peter, in the Cappella della Colonna. His pontificate lasted 23 years and 10 months.

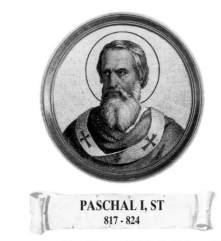

STEPHEN IV
816 - 817

PASCHAL I, ST
817 - 824

97 – Born in Rome. Elected June 22, 816 - died January 24, 817. He tried to prevent internal turmoil by introducing an oath for the Emperor whereby he had to be faithful to the Pope. In Rheims, he consecrated Lodovic King of the Franks together with his wife Ermenengarde. He founded the monastery of St. Pressede, where Greek monks had to sing psalms day and night. He is buried in the Vatican Grottoes. His pontificate lasted only 7 months and 2 days

98 – Born in Rome. Elected January 25, 817 - died February 11, 824. Immediately after his election, Lodovic the Pious donated Sardinia and Corsica to him. He committed himself to the discovery of catacombs, transferring the mortal remains of more than 2,300 martyrs. He also provided help to the Christians from Palestine and Spain in the fight against the Saracens. Three out of the four cardinals consecrated during Paschal's pontificate became his successors, i.e. Valentine, Gregory IV and Sergius II. During his pontificate a huge fire damaged the Borgo and the flames nearly reached the Portico of St. Peter. He is buried in the Vatican Grottoes. His pontificate lasted about 7 years.

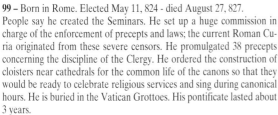

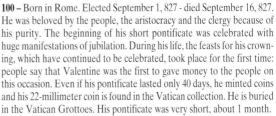

EUGENE II
824 - 827

VALENTINE
827

99 – Born in Rome. Elected May 11, 824 - died August 27, 827. People say he created the Seminars. He set up a huge commission in charge of the enforcement of precepts and laws; the current Roman Curia originated from these severe censors. He promulgated 38 precepts concerning the discipline of the Clergy. He ordered the construction of cloisters near cathedrals for the common life of the canons so that they would be ready to celebrate religious services and sing during canonical hours. He is buried in the Vatican Grottoes. His pontificate lasted about 3 years.

100 – Born in Rome. Elected September 1, 827 - died September 16, 827. He was beloved by the people, the aristocracy and the clergy because of his purity. The beginning of his short pontificate was celebrated with huge manifestations of jubilation. During his life, the feasts for his crowning, which have continued to be celebrated, took place for the first time: people say that Valentine was the first to gave money to the people on this occasion. Even if his pontificate lasted only 40 days, he minted coins and his 22-millimeter coin is found in the Vatican collection. He is buried in the Vatican Grottoes. His pontificate was very short, about 1 month.

GREGORY IV
827 - 844

SERGIUS II
844 - 847

101 – Born in Rome. Elected September 20, 827 - died January 11, 844. He set up a strong army, which was commanded by the Earl of Tuscany and defeated the Saracens five times in Africa. The latter, who had landed in Italy, destroyed Civitavecchia and Ostia and threatened Rome. In 834 he promulgated in Western Europe the feast of All Saints to be celebrated on the first day of November, which was introduced in Rome by St. Boniface IV. He ordered that each church had to have its own entrance and every priest had to abandon any other indecent occupation. He is buried in the Vatican Grottoes. His pontificate lasted 16 years.

102 – Born in Rome. Elected January 844 - died January 27, 847. During his pontificate, the Saracens besieged Rome, where they sacked St. Paul's and other churches. The Turks were definitively defeated in Gaeta. He restored the staircase of the Pretorium (Holy Stairs) in Jerusalem, which as you may know was brought to Rome by St. Helen, Constantine's mother. He is buried in the Vatican Grottoes. His pontificate lasted about 3 years.

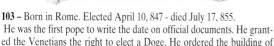

LEO IV, ST.
847 - 855

BENEDICT III
855 - 858

103 – Born in Rome. Elected April 10, 847 - died July 17, 855.
He was the first pope to write the date on official documents. He granted the Venetians the right to elect a Doge. He ordered the building of the walls surrounding the Leonine City and the Vatican hill. These walls, made of tufa and bricks, were up to 20 meters high: they had 24 towers like the one you can see on the Vatican hill. He ordered that the cardinals had to go twice a week to the Apostolic Palace to discuss Church matters; this was considered the first example of Congregation. Through one of his order, Leo IV introduced the aspersion, a rite which consists in sprinkling holy water on the faithful and on the works during the Sunday Mass etc. as a symbol of purification and blessing. He is buried in the Basilica of St. Peter, in the Cappella della Colonna. His pontificate lasted 8 years and 3 months.

104 – Born in Rome. Elected September 28, 855 - died April 17, 858. He was beloved by the people for his virtues but was firmly opposed by the Emperor and the Anti-pope Anastasius, whose pontificate lasted 1 month. He tried to gather all factions in the fight against the Saracens. He reluctantly accepted the pontificate and fasted three days before accepting the papal dignity. During his pontificate a pestilence broke out in Rome, which occluded one's throat with fluxion, causing the prompt death of people of any age and class. He is buried in the Vatican Grottoes. His pontificate lasted about 2 years and a half.

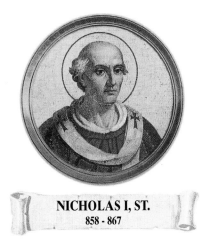

NICHOLAS I, ST.
858 - 867

HADRIAN II
867 - 872

105 – Born in Rome. Elected April 24, 858 - died November 13, 867. After serious disagreement with the Emperor Ludovic II, he co-operated with him to set up an army against the Saracens. He strongly defended the freedom of the Church against Photius. He introduced the Assumption Day celebrated on August 15th. Nicholas I considered the ring as a symbol of the consecrated union with the Church, the use of the wedding ring dates back to this period; in the past, Greek and Roman women used to wear a smooth ring as a talisman. During his pontificate, the Bulgarians were converted to Christianity: a mission was sent to the court of King Boris I. He was sanctified during the time of Urban VIII. He is buried in the Vatican Grottoes. His pontificate lasted 9 years and 7 months.

106 – Born in Rome. Elected December 14, 867 - died December 14, 872. It is worth mentioning the crowning of Alfred the Great, King of England (the first English King to be consecrated in Rome). He tried to settle the ever more serious disagreement among Catholic peoples. He called the 8th Ecumenical Council. He ordered that the monks who were consecrated Bishops should continue to wear the habit of their religious order. He is buried in the Vatican Grottoes. His pontificate lasted 5 years.

JOHN VIII
872 - 882

MARINUS I
882 - 884

107 – Born in Rome. Elected December 13, 872 - died December 16, 882. He faced the Saracens with only the help of Roman inhabitants, defeating them in Terracina. After the crowning, Charles the Gross refused to provide the help he had promised and the Pope was defeated by the Arabs; he was forced to pay a heavy tribute. He defined as impious all those who stole something from sacred places. Baronius and others write that he was the first to publish the rights and the pre-eminence of Cardinals. He died 10 years and 2 days after his election. He is buried in the Vatican Grottoes.

108 – Born in Gallese (Rome). Elected December 16, 882 - died May 15, 884. He firmly fostered Basil, the Eastern Emperor, to take action against schismatics. He supposedly died from poisoning after having tried to settle the disputes affecting Italy. He sent Formoso back to Porto, from where he had been exiled, and gave him his permission to come back to Rome. In Nonantola he met the Emperor Charles the Gross, obtaining his help against Guido of Spoleto, an enemy of the Church. At the request of Alfred of England, he exempted the "Schola Anglorum" of Rome from the payment of charges or taxes. He is buried in the Vatican Grottoes. He governed the Church for 1 year and 5 months.

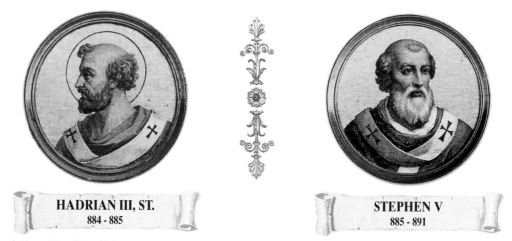

HADRIAN III, ST.
884 - 885

STEPHEN V
885 - 891

109 – Born in Rome. Elected May 17, 884 - died September 885. As soon as he was elected he confirmed the decisions taken by his predecessors with regard to the Emperor Photius. Following the invitation to go to France, that Charles the Gross had extended to him, he died in S. Cesareo sul Panaro during the journey, not far from the Abbey of Nonantola. He published two decrees: one concerning the election of the Pope and the other one related to the succession of Charles the Gross in the Kingdom of Italy; the first one was in favour of the liberty of Romans, since it was ordered that the elected Pope could be consecrated without the participation of the king or his ambassadors; and the second envisaged that in the next future the Kingdom of Italy was due to an Italian prince. He is buried in the monastery of Nonantola near Modena. His pontificate lasted about 1 year and 5 months.

110 – Born in Rome. Elected September 885 - died September 14, 891. After having heard the news about his election, he barricaded himself in his house, but after the doors were broken down he was forced to take office in St. Peter's. He prohibited the fire and water test during judgments and fostered arts and crafts. There are no monuments in Rome left to the memory of this Pope, who is supposed to have ordered the restoration of the Basilica of SS. Apostoli, the parish of his family. He is buried in the Vatican Grottoes. His pontificate lasted about 6 years.

FORMOSUS
891 - 896

BONIFACE VI
896

111 – Born in Ostia. Elected October 6, 891 - died April 4, 896. When he was a cardinal he was excommunicated by John VIII for having crowned Arnolfus King of Italy, who afterwards became Emperor of Germany. Thanks to him the Bulgarians were converted to Christianity. Formosus' true name was Damasus, a name that was given to him because of his rare elegance. He used to wear a cilice and was a vegetarian, he never ate meat nor drank wine. Formosus died after 4 years and 6 months of pontificate. His corpse was then defiled by Stephen VI, who considered Formosus an undeserving Pope because he had been condemned by John VIII; he was disinterred and put on trial, his body was maimed and he was thrown in the Tiber. The body was soon after recovered. At present, Formosus is buried in the Vatican Grottoes.

112 – Born in Rome. Elected April 896 - died in the same month. He came to the papal seat supported by the faction against Formosus and died 15 days later. The papal seat was at the mercy of Italian feudal vessels. His pontificate was very short: about 2 weeks, sometimes his name does not appear in the list of popes. He is buried in the Vatican Grottoes.

STEPHEN VI
896 - 897

ROMANUS
897

113 – Born in Rome. Elected May 22, 896 - died August 897. Submitted to internal quarrels, he had the corpse of Pope Formosus disinterred and thrown into the Tiber after an unfair trial. As a consequence of a popular insurrection, he was arrested and strangled in jail. Always in 897, during an earthquake, the old Basilica of San Giovanni in Laterano collapsed. He is buried in the Vatican Grottoes. His pontificate lasted about 1 year and 3 months.

114 – Born in Gallese (Rome). Elected August 897 - died in November of the same year. One of his first actions was that of rehabilitating the memory of Pope Formosus. He confirmed to Gerona the control of the islands of Majorca and Minorca. He died from poisoning. He is buried in the Vatican Grottoes. His pontificate was short, it lasted about 3 months.

THEODORE II
897

JOHN IX
898 - 900

115 – Born in Rome. Elected in December 897 - died in the same month. He ruled the Church for only 20 days, he transferred to the Vatican the mortal remains of Pope Formosus, pulled out from the Tiber. He died suddenly, probably from poisoning. As to the striking brevity of the pontificates of Stephen VI, Roman and Theodore II, Gregorovius said that the foul air of the profaned body of Formosus hung over the people, who passed by rapidly and fleetingly: it seemed that the angry spirit of Formosus rose over them. He is buried in the Vatican Grottoes.

116 – Born in Tivoli. Elected January 898 - died January 900.
He reaffirmed the supremacy of the Church over all its territories and Rome. In order to prevent certain struggles from occurring, he restored the imperial participation in the consecration of popes and to ensure the liberty of the pontifical election he wrote: from now on, we wish that the Pope, elected by the bishops and the whole clergy, be consecrated in the presence of the imperial commissioners and all the believers. He prohibited the sacking of bishops' and popes' palaces after their death, as usually occurred. He is buried in the Vatican Grottoes. His pontificate lasted about 2 years.

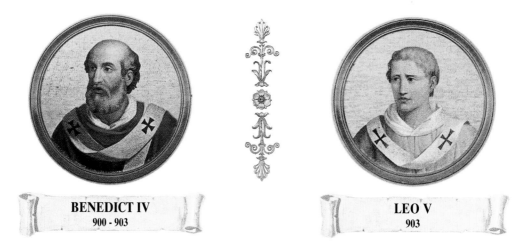

BENEDICT IV
900 - 903

LEO V
903

117 – Born in Rome. Elected February 1st, 900 - died July 903. Despite common corruption, he maintained the integrity of the Holy See. He looked for a way to find justice in the framework of intrigues and hate. He consecrated Emperor Louis of Burgundy. He provided his help and granted privileges to many monasteries, including the famous monastery of Fulda. At that time, there was such widespread ignorance that bishops had to question future priests to find out if they could read. He is buried in the Vatican Grottoes. His pontificate lasted about 3 years and 5 months.

118 – Born in Ardea. Elected in July 903 - died in September of the same year. Leo V was thrown out of the See and had to renounce in favour of Cardinal Christopher (anti-pope). During the numerous riots he was imprisoned and murdered. His body was burnt and the ashes thrown into the Tiber. His remains are buried in the Vatican Grottoes. His pontificate lasted about 2 months.

SERGIUS III
904 - 911

ANASTASIUS III
911 - 913

119 – Born in Rome. Elected January 29, 904 - died April 14, 911. He ordered the rebuilding of the Basilica of San Giovanni in Laterano, which had been destroyed by fire. He claimed and defended the rights of the Church against feudal vessels. For the first time, the coins dedicated to him have the tiara with the first crown (a sign of Spiritual Power) depicted on them (see also No. 193 and 200). He is buried in the Vatican Grottoes. His pontificate lasted about 7 years and 3 months.

120 – Born in Rome. Elected April 911 - died June 913. During his two years of pontificate he did not do much because of existing internal disagreement. He supported the pressure exerted by Berengarius I. He supposedly died by poison. He is buried in the Vatican Grottoes. His pontificate lasted about 2 years and 2 months.

LANDO
913 - 914

JOHN X
914 - 928

121 – Born in Sabina, he was elected June 913 - died February 914. He came to the papal seat as a result of the intrigues of one of the numerous factions. He died in mysterious circumstances after having succeeded, among other things, in restoring peace on civil strife. The brevity of these two pontificates, that of Lando and his predecessor Anastasius III, is apparently due to their tragic end caused by opposing factions. He is buried in the Vatican Grottoes. His pontificate lasted about 7 months.

122 – Born in Tossignano, he was elected March 914 - died May 928. He was elected as a result of intrigues and condemned the authors. He marched against the Saracens and surprisingly defeated them on the Garigliano. When he conducted the army, people said he behaved as a Pope and General at the same time. He was murdered in jail since he did not want to accept shady intrigues. He is buried in the Basilica of San Giovanni in Laterano. His pontificate lasted 14 years and 2 months.

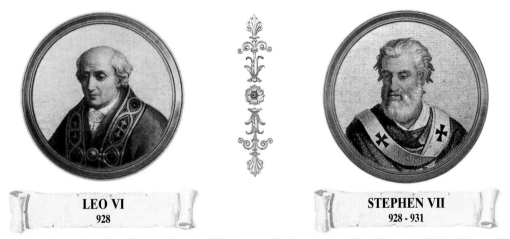

LEO VI
928

STEPHEN VII
928 - 931

123 – Born in Rome, he was elected May 928 - died December 928. He was elected according to the will of powerful Marotia. He did his best to try to settle disputes in Rome. He fought against the Saracens and the cruel Hungarians and defeated them. He made arts, commerce and industries flourish again. During his pontificate, the Prefect of Rome was appointed together with two consuls and the tribune of the people. He is buried in the Vatican Grottoes. His pontificate lasted only 7 months.

124 – Born in Rome, Elected December 928 - died February 931. He was elected as a result of the powerful intrigues of the earls of Tuscolo when Rome was ruled by Marotia, the Marquise of Tuscia. He supported the monasteries of St. Vincenzo al Volturno, S. Gerardo di Bragne and two cenobies in Gaul. He is buried in the Vatican Grottoes. His pontificate lasted about 2 years and 2 months.

JOHN XI
931 - 935

LEO VII
936 - 939

125 – Born in Rome, Elected March 931 - died December 935. He tried to solve the terrible intrigues of his family. Even if he was elected thanks to the support provided by the latter, he condemned their lack of restraint. He died at the age of 29 after many tribulations. As a result of Alberigus intrigues (the Pope's brother), the Patriarch of Constantinople and his successors were given the pallium ,which in turn was granted to all the Greek bishops without the intervention of popes. He is buried in the Basilica of San Giovanni in Laterano. His pontificate lasted almost 5 years.

126 – Born in Rome. Elected January 3, 936 - died July 13, 939. He reformed and reorganised monasticism and also ordered the rebuilding of the ancient Cenoby near the church of San Paolo Fuori le Mura in Rome. He informed French and German bishops about the phenomenon of wizards and fortune-tellers, who were supposed to perform easy prodigies. He invited Odonus to Rome, the Abbot of Cluny, and with his help he succeeded in restoring peace between Albericus and Hugo of Provence. He is buried in the Vatican Grottoes. His pontificate lasted about 3 years and 6 months.

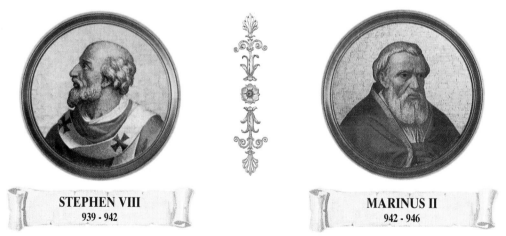

STEPHEN VIII
939 - 942

MARINUS II
942 - 946

127 – Born in Rome. Elected July 14 939 - died October 942. He supported Louis IV of Overseas against the rebellion of Frank vessels. He tried to convert the Eastern and Western powers to the holy principles of the Gospels. He suffered the supremacy of Albericus II, a tyrant of Rome, and of supporters, since they enjoyed the imperial preference. The face of Stephen VIII was so cruelly disfigured and wounded by them with deep cuts that he did not have the courage to present himself in public. He is buried in the Vatican Grottoes. His pontificate lasted 3 years and 5 months.

128 – Born in Rome. Elected October 30, 942 - died May 946. His life was irreproachable despite a period of turmoil. He fostered arts, reorganised corporations and made Rome become the capital of morality. He modified many of the rules regulating religious orders. In 1883, at the feet of the Palatine, in Vesta atrium, a deposit of silver Anglo-Saxon coins, surely sent from England to Rome as "denarius Sancti Petri", was discovered. Apart from the coins, also the rare fibula of a cappa pluvialis was found, bearing the inscription "Domno Marino Papa". This fibula may have been the symbol of a vestarius of the Roman Church. He is buried in the Vatican Grottoes. His pontificate lasted about 3 years and 6 months.

AGAPITUS II
946 - 955

JOHN XII
955 - 964

129 – Born in Rome. Elected May 10 946 - died October 955. He made every possible effort in order to improve the moral conditions of the clergy and with the help of Otto I from Germany he partially restored peace in Italy. Aroldus, King of Denmark, was converted to Christianity. Thanks to Agapitus II, the Papacy started a new life, resumed relations with foreign countries, which were not held by his predecessors. He is buried in the Basilica of San Giovanni in Laterano. His pontificate lasted about 9 years and 6 months.

130 – Born in Rome. Elected December 16, 955 - died May 14, 964. Since he was bold and brave he claimed the temporal rights of the Church. He reconstituted the Holy Roman Empire by crowning Otto I from Germany, who subsequently dethroned him. Otto I introduced the bishops-earls. By choosing the name of John XII instead of Octavianus, he introduced the habit of changing the Christian name, which afterwards became common among popes. John XII was the first Pope to commence relations with the Germans. He approved the German archdiocese of Magdeburg, which planned to send missionaries to the Slavic and Russian communities, where disputes among Byzantine Catholic and Orthodox were taking place. He is buried in the Basilica of San Giovanni in Laterano. His pontificate lasted 8 years and 5 months.

LEO VIII
963 - 965

BENEDICT V
964 - 966

131 – Born in Rome. Elected December 6, 963 - died March 1st, 965. He was elected anti-pope by Otto I, after alternate relationships with his predecessor and his successor, Benedict V. He forbade lay people to enter the presbytery during solemn services. The dethroning of John was considered valid and therefore the election of Leo VIII is legitimate.

132 – Born in Rome. Elected May 22, 964 - died July 4, 966. Otto I ordered his exile to Hamburg till the death of Leo VIII. After the death of the anti-pope, Otto I recognised the appointment, as a result of the pressures coming from Franks, Germans and Romans. He died in the name of sanctity in Hamburg. His pontificate lasted about 2 years and 2 months. It is necessary to say that if Leo VIII was a legitimate pope, then Benedict V was an anti-pope: on the other hand, both received the imperial legitimisation and an ecclesiastic confirmation. The period was gloomy and it is difficult to define with certainty the positions of the popes, and to establish the precise chronology of the pontifical succession. He is buried in the Vatican Grottoes.

JOHN XIII
965 - 972

BENEDICT VI
973 - 974

133 – Born in Rome. Elected October 1, 965 - died September 6, 972. He was imprisoned for a period of 10 months by the supporters of an opponent faction and was freed with the help of Otto I, who disseminated Christianity in Poland and Bohemia. He introduced the use of blessing and giving a name to bells: he blessed those of the Basilica Liberiana, giving them a name: one of the bells was called John. Strong and learned, he reorganised religious orders. He is buried in the Roman Basilica of S. Paolo Fuori le Mura. His pontificate lasted almost 7 years.

134 – Born in Rome. Elected January 19, 973 - died June 974. He converted the Hungarian people to Christianity. After the death of Otto I, the anti-German faction took power and besieged Castel S. Angelo. Benedict was imprisoned and murdered; he was strangled in the fortress of Castel S. Angelo and his body was thrown in the Tiber; it was immediately pulled out and buried in the Vatican Grottoes. We still have a letter written by Benedict VI and addressed to Frederick, Bishop of Salzburg, and to his Provincials, through which he gives him the office of vicar-apostolic in the Noricum and in the Pannonia, prohibiting to all the bishops of those provinces to wear the Pallium. His pontificate lasted about 1 year and a half.

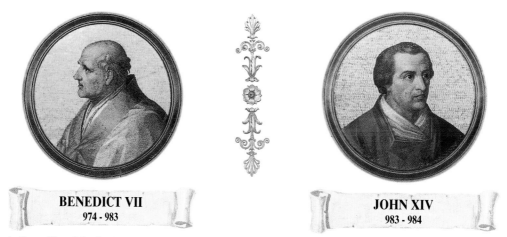

BENEDICT VII
974 - 983

JOHN XIV
983 - 984

135 – Born in Rome. Elected October 974 - died July 10, 983. He was a man endowed with wonderful gifts, who tried to stem immoral behaviour and the terrible ignorance widespread in Italy and the Christian world. He also fostered the development of agriculture. In the cloister of the abbey of Santa Scolastica in Subiaco there is a stone bearing an inscription written in rough letters, which states that this Pope consecrated the new church of the convent in 981. In the church of Santa Croce in Gerusalemnme, near Porta Maggiore, there is a memorial stone in his name. His pontificate lasted 8 years and 9 months.

136 – Born in Pavia. Elected December 983 - died August 20, 984. He was a very strong man with very rare qualities, and was elected as a result of unpleasant intrigues. Back to Rome, Francone ordered his arrest and made him starve to death in the prisons of Castel S. Angelo. After his election he changed his Christian name from Peter into John: he did this to show his respect towards St. Peter, the first Pope. Soon afterwards, Francone the anti-pope Boniface VII died and his body became the object of cruel outrage, dragged along the streets and finally thrown at the feet of Marcus Aurelius equestrian statue, which was once located in S. Giovanni in Lateran's square. The pontificate of John XIV lasted only 8 months. The day after his death merciful clerics buried him in the Vatican Grottoes.

JOHN XV
985 - 996

GREGORY V
996 - 999

137 – Born in Rome. Elected August 985 - died March 996. Caught in the snare of abuses, he was forced to look for shelter in Tuscany. He solved the disagreement affecting the church of Reims. He was the first Pope to carry forward the trial and the canonisation of a Saint: Ulderich, archbishop of Augsburg, who was made saint on decision of a Lateran synod. This was the first example of canonisation performed by a Pope. He is buried in the Vatican Grottoes. His pontificate lasted about 10 years and 7 months.

138 – Born in Saxony. Elected May 3, 996 - died November 11, 999. In the Basilica of St. Peter, he crowned his cousin Otto III, but after Otto went back to Germany, Gregory V was forced to leave Rome because of the threat represented by Crescentium, who opposed him with an anti-pope. Otto III came to the aid of the Pope; the anti-pope escaped from Rome and Crescentium was beheaded in Castel S. Angelo. He introduced the commemoration of the dead. He transferred St. Lucille's mortal remains to S. Maria Nuova in Rome. He is buried in the Vatican Grottoes. His pontificate lasted 2 years and 9 months.

SILVESTER II
999 - 1003

JOHN XVII
1003

139 – Born in Auvergne (France). Elected April 2, 999 - died May 12, 1003. He tried to stem immoral behaviour. He was extremely learned and introduced the use of Arab numbers. His pontificate crossed the threshold of the famous year 1000, which was considered crucial for the Last Judgment: people used to say: one thousand and not one thousand more. He is said to have invented the balance-wheel, which was used till 1640 and then replaced by the pendulum clock. He was the only Pope keen to astronomy and mathematics. He was also the first Pope to think about crusades, fostering princes and nations to start an allied war to free the Holy Land and Eastern Christians. He is buried in San Giovanni in Laterano. His pontificate lasted about 4 years and 1 month.

140 – Born in Rome. Elected June 1003 - died December 1003. His election took place in a period of serious disorders which followed the death of Otto II from Germany. We do not have significant information concerning his short pontificate. He is buried in San Giovanni in Laterano. His pontificate lasted about 5 months and 25 days.

JOHN XVIII
1004 - 1009

SERGIUS IV
1009 -1012

141 – Born in Rome. Elected January 1004 - died July 1009. He resumed the relationship, even if for a short period, between the Greek and the Latin church, and committed himself to making Christianity known among barbarians and pagans. He set up the bishopric of Bramberg. When the archbishop from Canterbury came to Rome to receive the Pallium, not only did he grant it to him but in front of the Senate, he actually took his stole off and gave it to him, saying he was worthy to wear it. He is buried in the Basilica of S. Paolo Fuori le Mura. His pontificate lasted about 5 years and 7 months.

142 – Born in Rome. Elected July 31, 1009 - died May 12, 1012. He changed his Christian name, for it was Peter. He maintained friendly relationships with Eastern and Western Emperors. He uselessly tried to stem immoral behaviour. He prevented the destruction of the Holy Sepulchre. He granted many benefits to Benedictine monasteries, the religious order to which he belonged before being elected. Sergius IV recognised the Camaldolensian order and the feudation of the famous monastery in Umbria operated by St. Romuald (1012); he then granted the investiture to the castles of roman country. He is buried in the Basilica of San Giovanni in Laterano. His pontificate lasted about 2 years and 10 months.

BENEDICT VIII
1012 - 1024

JOHN XIX
1024 - 1032

143 – Born in Rome, he was elected May 18, 1012 - died April 9, 1024. Given the opposition he encountered at the moment of his election, he asked for the assistance of Henry II, who was crowned in Rome. He promulgated laws against simony and duels. He ordered that churchmen could not marry. The use of the golden globe dates back to the period of Benedict VIII, the sceptre which he showed to Henry II at the moment of the crowning among all the insignia of the empire. It was a golden pommel covered by a cross. He is buried in the Vatican Grottoes. His pontificate lasted about 12 years

144 – Born in Rome. Elected May 1024 - died 1032. In Rome he crowned Emperor Conrad II from Germany. He did not give in to the unjustified demands put forward by the court of Byzantium. He protected Guido of Arezzo, the inventor of the musical notes, the names of which correspond to the first syllables of a psalm. The people from Constantinople begged Pope John XIX to allow their Church to have a universal character for the East; the ancient disagreement between Greek and Latin Churches was resumed by his refusal. He is buried in the Vatican Grottoes. His pontificate lasted about 8 years.

BENEDICT IX
1032 - 1044

SILVESTER III
1045

SILVESTER III, was declared a legitimate Pope by the 1947 revision. His official portrait is missing.

145 – Born in Rome. Elected in1032 - after having been dethroned in 1044, he looked for shelter in the monastery of Grottaferrata. He came to the papal seat when he was 12 (maybe 18). He ordered the King of Bohemia to bring back to Prague the mortal remains of St. Adalbert. Benedict IX was elected three times. Cardinal Hergenroother said he was endowed with practical sense and would have become an excellent pope thanks to his education and his ability to stifle emotions.

146 – Born in Rome. Elected January 20, 1045 - died February 10, 1045. He was replaced for a short period by Benedict IX, who excommunicated him, since he was considered an anti-pope. Despite numerous controversies, the Church recognised him as a legitimate Pope. There is no information about his death. He was elected on January 20, 1045 and was dethroned on February 10: 20 days later by the earls of Tuscolo, when Benedict IX came back to Rome. Silvester III looked for shelter in Sabina and was officially dethroned by the synod of Sutri in 1046. He is buried in the Vatican Grottoes.

BENEDICT IX
1045

GREGORY VI
1045 - 1046

147 – Elected for the second time September 10, 1045, he renounced the office on May 1st, 1045. After 20 days he was dethroned again as a result of economic and political interests and corruption. This all took place during the Middle Ages. After two months of struggle, Benedict IX came back to the papal seat to which he was entitled but he left it once again twenty days later in favour of Gregory VI, after receiving a large sum of money.

148 – Born in Rome. Elected May 5, 1045 - died December 20, 1046. He replaced the talked-of Benedict IX. He personally took the command of the army to fight against invaders. He was forced to abdicate. He supposedly set up the pontifical army, which had to free the territories of the Church from invaders. He was the first of the great Popes of the Reform. He is buried in the Vatican Grottoes. His pontificate lasted about 1 year and a half.

CLEMENT II
1046 - 1047

BENEDICT IX
1047 - 1048

149 – Born in Saxony. Elected December 25, 1046 - died October 9, 1047. He was worried about the arrogance showed by bishops-earls, as a result of relentless struggles with vessels; he managed to overcome the resistance of bishop Aribert from Milan, creating the famous "Carroccio". In Germany, he canonized St. Viborata, a Hungarian martyr. He was the second German Pope. He is supposed to have used the coat of arms for the first time. He is the only Pope to be buried in Germany, in fact he died in this country and his body lies in Bramberg in a richly decorated sarcophagus. His pontificate lasted about 10 months.

150 – Elected for the third time November 8, 1047, he renounced to his office on July 17, 1048. He followed the advice of St. Bartholomew and after eight months he resigned. Repenting his immoral life, he spent his last days as a monk in the convent of San Basilio in Grottaferrata, where he died and was buried.

DAMASUS II
1048

LEO IX, ST.
1049 - 1054

151 – Born in Bavaria. Elected July 17, 1048 - died August 9, 1048. He took the place of Benedict IX according to the will of Emperor Henry III from Germany, since Aliardus, Bishop of Lyon, had renounced the tiara. He retired to Palestrina where he died after only 23 days of pontificate. He is buried in the Basilica of S. Lorenzo Fuori le Mura in Rome.

152 – Born in Egnisheim (Alsazia). Elected March 12, 1049 - died April 19, 1054. He was freely elected by the clergy and the Roman people. Once arrived to Rome, he wanted to come to the papal seat on bare feet as a symbol of humility. He excommunicated Michele Cerulario who caused the schism of the Greek and Latin churches. He accepted the idea expressed by the reforming programme that the Pope should be elected by the single dignitaries of the church, called cardinals. The idea of Leo IX was definitely adopted 10 years later by Nicholas II. When he was 50, he started to study the Greek language in order to refute the writings of Greek schismatics. He is buried in the left transept of the Basilica of St. Peter. His pontificate lasted 5 years and 2 months.

VICTOR II
1055 - 1057

STEPHEN IX
1057 - 1058

153 – Born in Bavaria. Elected April 16, 1055 - died June 28, 1057. He was elected after one year of vacant office. He received the abjuration from Berengarius. He blessed Henry III at the point of death. Following the rules established by his predecessor, he made the Church thrive. One of his first actions was that of sending cardinal Ildebrando Aldobrandeschi to France with the task of calling councils and fight against the numerous heresies. He is buried in Ravenna in Santa Reparata. His pontificate lasted 2 years and 3 months.

154 – Born in Lorraine. Elected August 3, 1057 - died March 29, 1058. As soon as he was elected he tried to raise the moral behaviour of the clergy. He was surrounded by distinguished and important councillors who supported him in politics. He prohibited marriages between kinsmen. Stephen IX is the last of the five German popes who came to the papal seat after Clement II. He invited cardinal Ildebrando Aldobrandeschi to push Henry IV, who was still tutored by his mother, to stop the trade of ecclesiastic dignities, which was very intense in Germany both with regard to simony and abuses of power. He is buried in the Cathedral of Florence. His pontificate lasted about 8 months.

NICHOLAS II
1059 - 1061

ALEXANDER II
1061 - 1073

155 – Born in Burgundy. Elected January 24, 1059 - died July 27, 1061. He called a synod in Rome where he prohibited the appointment of bishops without papal authorisation and he decided that the election of the Pope was reserved only to cardinals-bishops (dioceses) and to cardinals-priests (parishes). This was the most important action taken by Nicholas II and this decree made the College of Roman Cardinals become a real ecclesiastic senate. He is buried in the Cathedral of Florence. His pontificate lasted 2 years and 2 months.

156 – Born in Milan, he was not elected in Rome, but in Terracina October 1st, 1061 - died April 21, 1073. His activity was religious rather than political. He took action in favour of the reform of the French Clergy. He was not recognised by the German empire and Henry IV opposed to him Onorius II as an anti-pope, causing turmoil and wars. People use to say that the Romans once saw four big camels walking along the streets of Rome, which Pope Alexander II received by Earl Ruggero, governor of Sicily. He is buried in the Grottoes of the St. Peter's Basilica. His pontificate lasted 11 years and 6 months.

GREGORY VII, ST.
1073 - 1085

VICTOR III, BL.
1086 - 1087

157 – Born in Tuscany. Elected April 22 1073 - died May 25, 1085. The council issued the "Dictatus Papae": only the Pope is universal; nobody can judge him; he is the only one who can release from oath. Henry IV, who was excommunicated, went to Canossa wearing a frock and begged for forgiveness: after three days during which the repentant Henry IV walked barefoot along the walls of Canossa, the Pope said, "that's enough" and so he was forgiven. He established that only the Supreme Hierarch could be called Pope. Gregory VII is the Pope of Canossa. He planned and promoted a transformation, which resulted in the Establishment of the "Licet de Vitanda", promulgated by Alexander III (170) according to which the election was reserved only to cardinals. He was buried in the Church of St. Matteo in Salerno. He was made saint in 1606. His pontificate lasted 12 years and 1 month.

158 – Born in Montecassino. Elected May 24, 1086 - died September 16, 1087. Four days after the election he looked for shelter in Montecassino. He was then re-elected and forced to come back to Rome and be consecrated. He excommunicated the Anti-pope Clemens III, and chose the fortified Tiberine island as his residence. He is supposed to have ordered the building of the Borgo near St. Peter, which now bears the name Victor. When he was a monk, S. Pier Damiani defined him: the Archangel of monks. He was one of the most distinguished men of his era and is mentioned among the scholars of the time. He was also very keen to sacred chants. He is buried in Montecassino. His pontificate lasted 1 year and 4 months.

URBAN II, BL.
1088 - 1099

PASCHAL II
1099 - 1118

159 – Born in France. Elected March 12, 1088 - died July 29, 1099. The Conclave was held in Velletri, because the anti-pope Clement III was settled in Rome. He declared war to the unfaithful and proclaimed the first crusade. He established the "Cease fire of God". A short break between battles to bury the dead. Goffredo di Buglione was appointed first commander; on July 15th the Christian army reached Jerusalem, and this event inspired Torquato Tasso in the composition of his poem entitled "Gerusalemme liberata": his scream "God wants it", was known all over Europe. During the council of Clermont, the Angelus Domini was introduced. He is buried in the Vatican Grottoes. His pontificate lasted 11 years and 4 months.

160 – Born in Bieda (Ravenna). Elected August 14, 1099 - died January 21, 1118. The struggle for the supremacy of the Pope or of the Emperor forced him to go to exile. Henry V succeeded in being crowned with the right of investiture. S. Maria del Popolo was built in the place where people said it was possible to see the ghost of Nero. In this church you might also find a Madonna attributed to St. Lucas, which would therefore date back to the same period of the famous polish "Black Madonna". During his pontificate, and more specifically in 1110, the military group of the Knights of Rodi of the Sacred Order of Malta was created. His body was buried in the Lateran. His pontificate lasted about 17 years and 5 months.

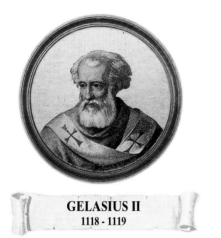

GELASIUS II
1118 - 1119

CALLISTUS II
1119 - 1124

161 – Born in Gaeta. Elected March 10, 1118 - died January 28, 1119. He was assailed in the Church of the Lateran and was imprisoned by the rebel Cencio Frangipane. After having been freed by Genoese mariners he looked for shelter in Gaeta, from where he came back to Rome dressed as a pilgrim . He moved to Cluny as a consequence of a turmoil of Roman nobles and never came back to Rome. People say that at the point of death, he took the pontifical insignia off, put the frock on and wanted to die on the ground. He was buried in the monastery of Cluny. His pontificate lasted a little longer than 9 months.

162 – Born in Burgundy. Elected February 8 1119 - died December 13, 1124. He signed the agreement published in Worms concerning the right of the popes to appoint cardinals. He called the 9th Ecumenical Council and proclaimed the 2nd Crusade. He was elected in Cluny and accepted the confirmation from the cardinals who remained in Rome, where messengers were sent; therefore, also the election of this Pope was held in Rome. We owe to Callistus II the end of the struggles for investitures, started by Gregory VII and Henry IV. He died suddenly in the Lateran Palace and was buried in the Basilica. His pontificate lasted 5 years and 10 months.

HONORIUS II
1124 - 1130

INNOCENT II
1130 - 1143

163 – Born in Fiagnano. Elected December 21, 1124 - died February 13, 1130. He resumed relations with almost all European countries fighting against the Saracens. During his pontificate, the famous factions of the Guelphs (in favour of the Pope) and the Ghibellines (in favour of the Emperor) were created. Since it was not possible to elect the successor of the Pope if the latter was not buried, the body of Honorius, still warm, was put into a temporary grave in the Convent of San Gregorio al Celio. He was then transferred to the Lateran. His pontificate lasted 5 years and 2 months.

164 – Born in Rome. Elected February 23, 1130 - died September 24, 1143. Soon after his election he was forced to escape. Lothar from Saxony brought him back to Rome, kissed his foot and lead his she-mule in the procession in exchange for the crowning. He called the 10th Ecumenical Council, the II Lateran, and dissolved the "Agapete" (community of women working for churchmen, currently called priest's housekeepers). He was at first buried in the La teran, but seven years later his body was transferred to S. Maria in Trastevere. His pontificate lasted about 13 years and 7 months.

CELESTINE II
1143 - 1144

LUCIUS II
1144 - 1145

165 – Born in Città di Castello. Elected October 3, 114 - died March 8, 1144. With the aid of St. Bernard, he settled the internal disputes of the Church. He tried to stop the war between Scotland and England, but did not succeed in obtaining peace in Italy. He withdrew the excommunication of Louis VII, King of France. Platina says he was the first Pope to be elected without the participation of the people. The so-called "St. Malachi's prophecies" by, the archbishop of Armagh in Ireland, date back to this period. He is buried in the Basilica of San Giovanni in Laterano. His pontificate lasted about 5 months.

166 – Born in Bologna. Elected March 12, 1144 - died February 15, 1145. He came to the papal seat in a period of turmoil caused by Arnaldo of Brescia. His pontificate was characterised by two events: Portugal was conquered by Henry of Burgundy, who defeated the Arabs, and was transformed into a kingdom and proclaimed vessel territory of the Church by Alphonse I and the creation of the communes all over Italy, an historical event of great importance. The creation of the so-called communes marked the end of the Middle Ages. While he was trying to settle a serious popular turmoil he was hit by a stone and died. He is buried in San Giovanni in Laterano. His pontificate lasted about 11 months.

EUGENE III, BL.
1145 - 1153

ANASTASIUS IV
1153 - 1154

167 – Born in Montemagro (Pisa). Elected February 8, 1145 - died July 8, 1153. He was forced to leave Rome a couple of times. He gave way to the already proclaimed 2nd Crusade. He established the Sacred College. He started the building of the "Pontifical Palace". He accepted the Knights of St. John of Jerusalem (of Malta). He refused to accept to his court the youths who paid too much attention to their curly hair. Eugene III used to wear a woolen frock and the cilice and slept on the ground. He was the first to talk about pontifical vacations and had a palace built in Segni. He is buried in the Vatican Grottoes. Eugene, whose pontificate lasted 8 years and 5 months, was beatified by the Church. His beatification was confirmed on October 3rd, 1872.

168 – Born in Rome. Elected July 12, 1153 - died December 3, 1154. He was elected Pope when he was already old. In the same year of his election, St. Bernard of Chiaravalle died. Carindal Brek-Pear was his councillor, who afterwards became Hadrian IV. Thanks to the mildness of his attitude, he succeeded in restoring peace in the temporal dominions of the Church. When Rome was hit by a serious famine, he was called the "Father of Rome and the Apostle of Charity". People say that his mortal remains were put in the urn where St. Helen was resting. He is buried in the Basilica of San Giovanni in Laterano. His pontificate lasted about 1 year and 5 months.

HADRIAN IV
1154 - 1159

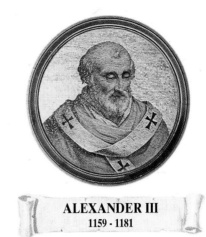

ALEXANDER III
1159 - 1181

169 – Born in Langley (England). Elected December 5, 1154 - died September 1st, 1159. He was a supporter of pontifical supremacy. At the meeting held in Sutri, Barbarossa refused to hold the bridle of the Pope's mule and he refused him the kiss of forgiveness. Arnold of Brescia was burned according to an order given by the Pope, who had his ashes thrown in the Tiber; according to other sources, Frederick II rather than Hadrian ordered this terrible torture. He was the first and the only English Pope. Before dying, he recommended his old and poor mother to the charity of the church of Canterbury. He was buried in an ancient urn made of red granite, in the dungeons of the Basilica of St. Peter. In 1607, when the sepulchre was opened, he was found intact and dressed with dark habits. His pontificate lasted almost 5 years.

170 – Born in Siena. Elected September 20, 1159 - died August 20, 1181. He excommunicated Barbarossa because of his evil actions, supported the Lombard League, and defeated him in Legnano with the famous "Carroccio". He called the 11th Ecumenical Council. He reserved to the Pope the right to canonisation. He definitively decided through the bull "Licet et Vitanda" issued in 1179, that the Pope had to be elected only by cardinals, without any other influence from the clergy or the people, and with a majority of at least two thirds (this last provision was left unchanged until Paul VI, who introduced the second ballot). He was buried in San Giovanni in Laterano. His pontificate lasted almost 22 years.

LUCIUS III
1181 - 1185

URBAN III
1185 - 1187

171 – Born in Lucca. Elected in Velletri September 6, after one day of office vacancy, 1181 - died September 25, 1185. He planned and promoted a statute (November 4th, 1184), which had to contain the rules and functions for a more rapid repression than the public accusation against heretics, and that lead to the creation of the Tribunal of the Holy Office (Paul III, 220). He was buried in the Cathedral of Verona. His pontificate lasted almost 4 years and 2 months.

172 – Born in Milan. Elected December 1st, 1185 - died October 20, 1187. He was elected in Verona and chose this city as his pontifical residence. When he was a cardinal, he created the "Lombard League". He opposed the abuses of Barbarossa and died of grief when the Saracens occupied Jerusalem. Urban III never came to Rome. He is buried in the Cathedral of Ferrara. His pontificate lasted about 1 year and 10 months.

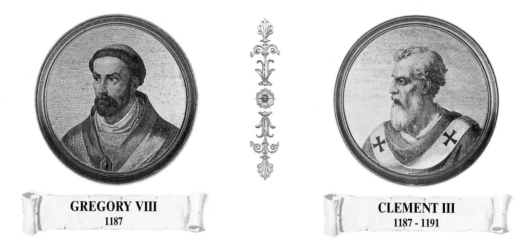

GREGORY VIII
1187

CLEMENT III
1187 - 1191

173 – Born in Benevento. Elected October 25, 1187 - died December 17, 1187. He was elected in Ferrara. Accepted by Barbarossa, he succeeded in settling the disputes between the Church and the Empire, thanks to a longer pontificate. He helped the Christians in the Holy Land, who were oppressed by the unfaithful. He was buried in the Cathedral of Pisa and on occasion of the fire that broke out in this Cathedral on October 15th 1595, his mortal remains were destroyed and part of the monument was burnt. His pontificate lasted 1 month and 27 days.

174 – Born in Rome. Elected December 20, 1187 - died March 1191. He restored peace in Rome after 60 years during which time the Popes had been forced to leave the city. He promoted the 3rd Crusade, in which also the English King Richard the Lionhearted participated. At the end of this crusade, the Christian Kingdom of Cyprus was established and Clement obtained a strip of Palestine coast and the permission to visit the Holy Sepulchre that had been in the hands of Sultan Saladine since 1187. He is buried in the Basilica of San Giovanni in Laterano. His pontificate lasted 3 years and 3 months.

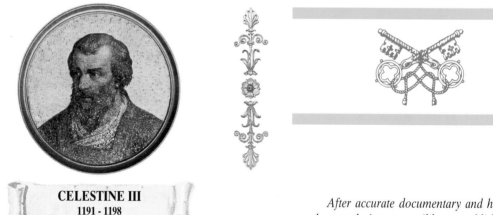

CELESTINE III
1191 - 1198

175 – Born in Rome. Elected April 14, 1191 - died January 8, 1198. He affirmed the indissolubility of marriage. He approved the Teutonic knight order, the main task of which was that of defending the pilgrims who went to the Holy Land. He also took action in order to regulate monasticism and decided, in an open and respectful decision, that the young boys who were destined to religious life, could freely change their mind once of age. After a long period of time, Celestine III was the only Pope to spend all the years of his pontificate in Rome. He was buried in the Basilica of San Giovanni in Laterano. His pontificate lasted about 6 years and 9 months.

After accurate documentary and historical research, it was possible to establish with certainty when the pontifical coat of arms was introduced.

Innocent III began the special collection of Papal coat of arms, which still continues today and characterises the family or house of origin, the written and sealed documents, as well as the works or monuments built upon request of the Pope.

176 – Born in Anagni. Elected February 22, 1198 - died July 16, 1216. A man of great qualities, he exerted a strong influence. He restored the temporal authority in the Pontifical States. He promoted the IV Crusade. He approved the Dominican and Franciscan orders. He called the 12th Ecumenical Council. He forbade churchmen to play cards. The use of keys as a Papal emblem dates back to this period. He accurately defined the issue of the ring, worn by cardinals and bishops; the engraved stone was used as a seal; Innocent decided that amethysts, sapphires, topazes and rubies were the stones to be used. He was buried in the Basilica of San Giovanni in Laterano. His pontificate lasted about 18 years and a half.

1198   1216
LOTARIO
DEI CONTI DI SEGNI

INNOCENT III
1198 - 1216

177 – Born in Rome. Elected July 24 - died February 8, 1227. He wrote the "Liber Censorium" on the rights of Popes and established the ceremonial for the election. He organised the 5th Crusade together with Andrew II of Hungary. Thanks to John I of Sweden, Christianity was extended to Estonia. He granted the Church of Santa Sabina in Rome to San Domenico, as well as the annexed palace in the garden of which you might still find the first orange-tree imported from Spain by Dominic himself. He was buried in S. Maria Maggiore. His pontificate lasted 10 years and 8 months.

ONORIO III

1216   1227
CENCIO SAVELLI

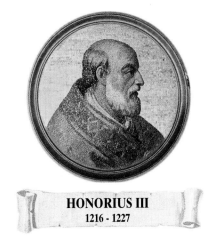

HONORIUS III
1216 - 1227

178 – Born in Anagni. Elected March 21, 1227 - died August 22, 1241. He excommunicated Frederick II for his demeanor. He instituted the "Holy Inquisition". He approved the collection of divine offices, called "breviary" and later modified by John XXIII in 1960. He organised the University of Paris through the Bull Parens Scientiarium and organised the 6th Crusade.. He canonized St. Francis of Assisi (1228), St. Anthony of Padua and St. Dominic of Guzman (1234). He is buried in the Vatican Grottoes. His pontificate lasted about 14 years and 6 months.

GREGORIO IX

1227   1241
UGOLINO
DEI CONTI DI SEGNI

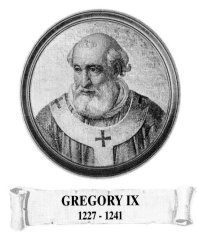

GREGORY IX
1227 - 1241

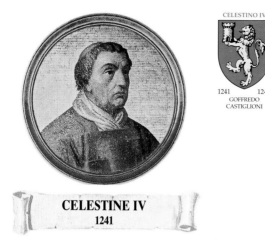

179 – Born in Milan. Elected October 28,1241 - died November 10, 1241. Because the cardinals did not come to an agreement, for this election, the Roman Senate "locked" them into the Palace of the Settinozio sul Celio. The word "Conclave" takes origin from this episode, and more specifically from the Latin expression "cum clave". After Celestine's death, the Holy See remained vacant for one year, eight months and 17 days since the cardinal, worried about the anger of Emperor Frederick II, who imprisoned almost all of them, could not elect his successor. He is buried in the Vatican Grottoes. His pontificate was one of the shortest: it lasted only 17 days.

CELESTINE IV
1241

180 – Born in Genoa. Elected June 28, 1243 - died July 7, 1254. He was elected in Anagni after two years of vacancy. He was a distinguished canonist. He called the 13th Ecumenical Council. He introduced the feast of the Visitation. He promoted the 7th Crusade together with St. Louis IX of France. In 1245 he granted to the cardinals the insignia of the red hat, as a symbol of their availability to give their blood for the church. Paul II then granted them the biretta and the skull-cap of the same colour. He proclaimed that the Coliseum was part of the dominion of the church. He forbade the Jews to have Christian wet-nurses or servants. He was buried in the Church of S. Restituita in Naples. His pontificate lasted 11 years and 6 months.

INNOCENT IV
1243 - 1254

181 – Born in Anagni. Elected December 20, 1254 - died May 25, 1261. He wrote about popular jurisprudence. He canonized Santa Chiara and confirmed the existence of St. Francis stigmata. He established the summary proceedings for heretics and condemned the "flagellants", those men who took their clothes off till the belt, put a cap on and took a whip. The Pope, worried about the diffusion of heretical sects, prohibited the processions, which ended in January 1261. He is buried in the Cathedral of Viterbo. His pontificate lasted 6 years and 5 months.

ALEXANDER IV
1254 - 1261

182 – Born in Troyes (France), he was surprisingly elected September 4, 1261 during the Conclave of Viterbo, in which he participated to pay his respects to the future Pope - died October 2, 1264. He confirmed the feast of the Corpus Domini to be celebrated 60 days after Easter and the hymns for the celebration of the feast were written by Thomas Aquinas, while the procession was established by John XXII (1316-1334). He began to write ordinal numbers on documents followed by his name "Pope Urban IV". He prohibited the burial in the Vatican Basilica of all those who had not received a pontifical authorisation. He was buried in the Cathedral of Deruta (Perugia). His pontificate lasted about 3 years.

URBANO IV

1261   1264
GIACOMO
PANTALÉON

URBAN IV
1261 - 1264

183 – Born in Saint Giles (France). Elected February 15, 1265 - died November 28, 1268. He excommunicated Conrad of Swabia but this did not avoid the occupation of Rome and Naples. Before becoming a priest and a bishop he was a man of the world. He lived and died in Viterbo. People say that a particular Breve was the first one to be sealed with the piscatory ring (papal ring, with reference to St. Peter). Clement IV belongs to the group of Popes who never came to Rome, since he spent his entire life in Viterbo. His pontificate lasted 3 years and 10 months.

CLEMENTE IV

1265   1268
GUIDO FOULQUOIS

CLEMENT IV
1265 - 1268

184 – Born in Piacenza. Elected March 27, 1272 - died January 10, 1276. After almost three years of vacancy because of disagreements within the Conclave of Viterbo, some men of the people took the roof off and put the cardinals on bread and water, forcing them to make a decision. He called the 14th Ecumenical Council. With the Bull "Ubi Periculum" (7.7.1274) he explained that after three days of conclave the lunch was reduced to two meals per day, one in the morning and the other one at night; after five days only bread, water and some wine were allowed. The provisions contained in the "Ubi Periculum" were then eased and finally eliminated, but the enclosure remained and is still used today. He was buried in the Cathedral of Arezzo. His pontificate lasted about 3 years and 10 months.

B. GREGORIO X

1272   1276
TEBALDO VISCONTI

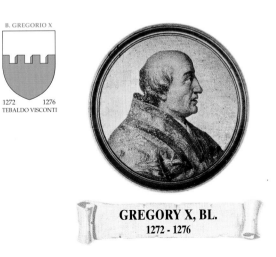

GREGORY X, BL.
1272 - 1276

B. INNOCENZO V

1276   1276
PIETRO DI
TARANTASIA

185 – Born in Sutron (Savoy). Elected February 22, 1276 - died June 22, 1276. The total enclosure was observed during his conclave. He diffused Christianity till the far-off Mongolia, baptising three ambassadors sent by the Great Khan. During this period, the struggles between Guelphs and Ghibellines and the opposed factions within these two groups were underway. He was the first Pope who belonged to the Dominican order. He died only 4 months after his election. He is buried in the Basilica of San Giovanni in Laterano.

INNOCENT V, BL.
1276

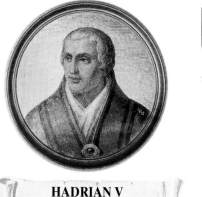

ADRIANO V

1276   1277
OTTOBONO
FIESCHI

186 – Born in Genoa. Elected July 11, 1276 - died August 8, 1276 after only 38 days of pontificate. He was not consecrated. He restored order in religious orders. He suspended the rules concerning the conclave issued by Gregory X. The mausoleum dedicated to this Pope was the first one to bear the family's coat of arms . This habit was then resumed when the sepulchre of Boniface VIII (Caetani) was built. He is buried in Viterbo, in the Church of San Francesco. His pontificate lasted 1 month and 9 days.

HADRIAN V
1276

GIOVANNI XXI

1276   1277
PIETRO IULIANI

187 – Born in Portugal. Elected September 20, 1276 - died May 20, 1277. Alphonsus II of Portugal promised him that all the churches of that kingdom and their profits would have been respected. He died during the collapse of his residential palace in Viterbo. Pietro Giuliano, that is to say John XXI, in order to allow the people to follow his valuable rules, wrote the famous "Treasure of the Poor", an actual real first aid treaty. He was buried in the Cathedral of San Lorenzo in Viterbo. His pontificate lasted about 8 months.

JOHN XXI
1276 - 1277

188 – Born in Rome. Elected December 26, 1277 - died August 22, 1280, in his villa at Soriano nel Cimino. He was the first Pope to live in the Vatican and had the famous gardens built. He sent missionaries to convert Tartar Kings. He came to an agreement with the city of Viterbo concerning the curia and forced the Municipality to appropriately furbish the Pontifical Palace, giving free residence to the cardinals and the members of the curia and sending away prostitutes and mediators. He had the famous "Passetto" built: an elevated corridor linking the Vatican to the fortress of Castel S. Angelo. He ordered the third series of portraits of the Popes in S. Paolo Fuori le Mura, deducting dates and physiognomy from ancient documents. He is buried in the Vatican Grottoes. His pontificate lasted about 2 years and 8 months.

NICCOLÒ III

1277　1280
GIOVANNI GAETANO ORSINI

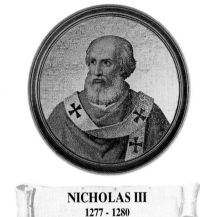

NICHOLAS III
1277 - 1280

189 – Born in France. Elected March 23, 1281 - died March 23, 1285. He tried to convey the sense of charity to the great and powerful of that period. During his pontificate, the famous revolution of the Sicilian Vespers broke out. Giuseppe Verdi wrote an opera in 5 acts, which was performed for the first time in Paris in 1855. He ordered the building of two pontifical palaces in Orvieto and Montefiascone, from where the stronghold takes origin. He is buried in the Cathedral of Perugia. His pontificate lasted 4 years and 1 month.

MARTINO IV

1281　1285
SIMONE DE BRION

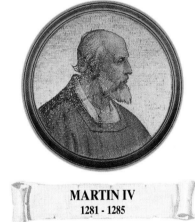

MARTIN IV
1281 - 1285

190 – Born in Rome. Elected May 20, 1285 - died April 3, 1287. His first action was that of restoring order in the Pontifical State. He fostered the University of Paris and tried to resume relations with the Greek Church; he also tried to come to an agreement with the Islamic people. He recognised the Carmelites. He was so tormented by gout that he had difficulty moving, and when he was saying Mass he needed some special devices to raise his hands and lift the Host. Paul III (1534-1549) transferred the body of Honorius IV to the Aracoeli Church, near his mother's grave. His pontificate lasted 2 years and 1 day.

ONORIO IV

1285　1287
GIACOMO SAVELLI

HONORIUS IV
1285 - 1287

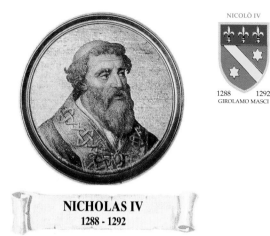

191 – Born in Ascoli. Elected February, 1288 - died April 4, 1292. He restored order in the court of Portugal and promoted the development of education, creating the University of Montpellier. He intensified missions and fought against the Saracens together with Genoa. He was the first Franciscan Pope. According to the portrait by Benozzo Golloli in St. Francis of Montefalco, Nicholas was tall and fat. He had the apse of S. Maria Maggiore built and decorated; Jacopo Torriti and Camerino produced the mosaics in the apse of San Giovanni in Laterano; finally, he laid the foundation stone of the Cathedral of Orvieto. He was buried in S. Maria Maggiore. His pontificate lasted 4 years and 2 months.

NICHOLAS IV
1288 - 1292

192 – Born in Isernia. Elected August 29, 1294 - died May 19, 1296. He was an extremely moral and simple man, and when he realised he had been merely used by the most powerful people of those gloomy Middle Ages he renounced the pontificate. He established that the newly elected Pope had the faculty to renounce the election. After his decision, to which he was lead also by the smart campaign carried forward by Cardinal Caetani, who was to become his successor with the name of Boniface VIII, he was confined into the Castle of Fumone, a small village of the Ciociaria near Ferentino, where he lived as a prisoner under harsh conditions. His body was transferred to the church of Collemaggio near Aquila. His pontificate lasted only 5 months.

CELESTINE V, ST.
1294

193 – Born in Anagni. Elected December 24, 1294 - died October 11, 1303. He was a great Pope. He celebrated for the first time the Holy Year (1300), which had to occur every 100 years. He founded the University "La Sapienza" in Rome. He was the patron of distinguished artists among whom Giotto. Philip the Fair, when he was about to be excommunicated, sent some of his followers to Anagni: Guglielmo Nogaret and Sciarra Colonna, breaking the doors of the town open, saw the Pope dressed with pontifical attires and sitting on the throne; historians say that is not true that Nogaret hit the Pope with his iron glove when he offered them "the head and the neck". Boniface supported the rights of the clergy but encountered the opposition of the kings of Europe. He added a second crown to the tiara, the "Regal Power" (see also 119 and 200). He is buried in the Vatican Grottoes. His pontificate lasted 8 years and 10 months.

BONIFACE VIII
1294 - 1303

194 – Born in Treviso. Elected October 27, 1303 - died July 7, 1304. He settled the serious dispute with the Kingdom of France. He was prosecuted by a group of conspirators and died from poisoning after having eaten figs, of which he was very fond. Since Benedict X was an anti-pope, he should have been called Benedict X but he refused this name because it had been attributed to an usurper. He was buried in the Church of San Domenico in Perugia. On April 24th 1736 he was beatified by Clement XII. His pontificate lasted about 8 months.

B. BENEDETTO XI

1303   1304
NICCOLÒ
BOCCASINI

BENEDICT XI, BL.
1303 - 1304

195 – Born in Willaudraut (France). Elected November 14, 1305 - died April 20, 1314. He was consecrated in Lyon and under the influence of Philip the Fair settled the residence of the Holy See in Avignon; this situation lasted 70 years. He called the 15th Ecumenical Council. He founded the University of Oxford, the University of Perugia and introduced the chairs of Hebraic, Syrian and Arab in the University of Bologna. He was elected by the conclave of Perugia, which lasted almost 11 months since the cardinals could not come to an agreement. He established his residence in Avignon. At the request of the king, he abolished the rich and powerful order of the Templars. He is buried in France, in Uzes. His pontificate lasted 8 years and 10 months.

CLEMENTE V

1305   1314
BERTRANDO DE GOT

CLEMENT V
1305 - 1314

196 – Born in Cahors (France). Elected September 5, 1316 - died December 4, 1334. He was elected in Lyon after a vacancy of two years. He introduced the Holy Trinity Holiday, the Tribunal of the Rota (the round table of judges) and ordered the building of the Pontifical Palace in Avignon. He reserved the office of the pontifical sacristan and confessor of the Pontifical Palaces to an Augustinian bishop. He intensified the missions to Ceylon, Nubia and among the Tartars. He introduced the Corpus Domini procession. He canonized Thomas of Aquinas and approved the Olivetan order. He was buried in the cathedral of Avignon. His pontificate lasted about 18 years and 4 months.

GIOVANNI XXII

1316   1334
GIACOMO DUESE

JOHN XXII
1316 - 1334

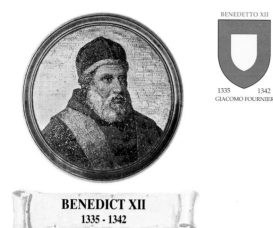

197 – Born in Saverdun (France). Elected January 8, 1335 - died April 25, 1342. He was forced by Philip VI to live in France who also took action in Roman affairs. He forced the bishops to have a residence and reformed the Benedictine, Franciscan and Dominican orders. Petrarque was crowned by him in Campidoglio on April 8th 1341. He published the "pragmatic sanction" of Frankfurt, through which he established that the appointment of the emperor did not need the pontifical placet. He was buried in the cathedral of Avignon. His pontificate lasted 7 years and 4 months.

BENEDICT XII
1335 - 1342

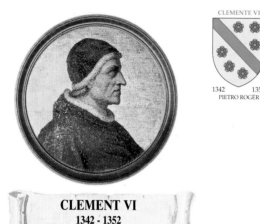

CLEMENTE VI

1342   1352
PIETRO ROGÉR

198 – Born in Maumont (France). Elected May 19, 1342 - died December 6, 1352. He was a very learned and good-hearted man. He bought the city of Avignon for 18,000 golden florins. He protected the Jews. He shortened the interval between holy years to 50 years and celebrated the 2nd one in 1350. In a letter written on November 2nd 1342, Clement VI recognised the custody of Holy places to Friars minors: in 1333 Robert, King of Naples, had obtained some rights in the Holy Land from the Sultan as a compensation for the numerous convents destroyed during the prosecutions of Saracens that took place in Palestine and Syria. He was buried in the monastery of La Chaise-Dieu, in the High Loire. His pontificate lasted 10 years and 7 months.

CLEMENT VI
1342 - 1352

INNOCENZO VI

1352   1362
STEFANO AUBERT

199 – Born in Braisahmont (France). Elected December 30, 1352 - died September 12, 1362. He made the Spanish Alornoz restore the order in the Pontifical State. He promoted arts and culture. He fortified Avignon with walls. He established that during the Vacancy of the See the cardinals were not entitled to issue laws aimed at limiting the authority of the Pope and abolished the already passed ones. Innocent VI, as you might see in two miniatures available in the Vatican archives, had a beard and was the only pope of the XIV and XV century to do so. Julius II was the first one to imitate him and renew the custom. He was buried in the Chapel of the Hospice of Villeneuve. His pontificate lasted about 9 years and 9 months.

INNOCENT VI
1352 - 1362

200 – Born in France. Elected November 6, 1362 - died December 19, 1370. He tried to return to Rome but after 3 years of troubles he came back to Avignon. He added the 3rd crown to the tiara (triregnum), the "Imperial Power"; the 2nd one was the "Regal Power" (Boniface VIII); the 1st one was the "Spiritual Power" (Sergius III). The Conclave for Urban V was the fourth ever held in France. On the day of the crowning he refused to solemnly appear riding on a horse, since he believed that the pontifical dignity had been exiled to Avignon. He ordered the rebuilding of the Basilica of San Giovanni in Laterano, destroyed in 1360; he decorated the major altar with the tabernacle and closed in silver busts the heads of St. Peter and St. Paul previously kept in the Sancta Sanctorum. He was buried in the Church of St. Victor in Marseilles. His pontificate lasted about 8 years and 2 months.

B. URBANO V

1362   1370
GUGLIELMO
DE GRIMOARD

URBAN V, BL.
1362 - 1370

201 – Born in Maumont (France). Elected January 5, 1371 - died February 26, 1378. Thanks to the intervention of St. Catherine he brought the Holy See back to Rome. The Roman Senate donated part of the Vatican hill to him. He included S. Maria Maggiore among the basilicas destined to the jubilee indulgence. Gregory realised that by staying in France he could not manage to preserve the unity of the Pontifical State. Therefore, despite the foreseeable oppositions of French bishops, he decided to return to Rome on January 17th 1377. On the very night in which Gregory XI died, March 26th 1378, the palace of Avignon was almost completely destroyed by fire. Gregory was the last French Pope. He is buried in the Church of Santa Francesca Romana. His pontificate lasted 7 years and 3 months.

GREGORIO XI

1371   1378
PIETRO ROGER
DE BEAUFORT

GREGORY XI
1371 - 1378

202 – Born in Naples. Elected April 18, 1378 - died October 15, 1389. This was the first conclave held in the Vatican. He was the last Pope to be elected without being a cardinal. The anti-pope Clement VII was defined Anti-Christ by St. Catherine of Siena. England, Germany, Hungary, Poland, Denmark, Sweden and Norway, Northern and Central Italy remained faithful to Urban VI. France, Scotland, Spain and the Kingdom of Naples were in favour of Clement VII, causing the schism that lasted 40 years. Historians agree on the fact that the Lutheran reform began in this period. He is buried in the Vatican Grottoes. His pontificate lasted 11 years and 6 months.

URBANO VI

1378   1389
BARTOLOMEO
PRIGNANO

URBAN VI
1378 - 1389

203 – Born in Naples. Elected November 1389 - died October 1st 1404. He did not solve the schismatic issue. Also the second anti-pope from Avignon refused a conciliation. He celebrated the 3rd and 4th Holy Year (1390-1400) during which time the "sect of the whites" was set up in Provence. He was skilled in chants and music. He was surrounded by Jewish doctors and surgeons. He was indomitable against anti-pope Benedict XIII, the Spanish Cardinal Pietro di Luna, called "the big snake". He was the first to make Castel S. Angelo become a real fortress, since he bore in mind what he was once told: "if you want to be the master of Rome you must prepare the Castle". He is buried in the Vatican Grottoes. His pontificate lasted almost 15 years.

BONIFACE IX
1389 - 1404

204 – Born in Sulmona. Elected November 11, 1404 - died November 6,1406. He was a learned but weak man, who tried to settle the serious schism and to improve the tragic conditions under which the State of the Church was living. He optimised the faculties of Greek and medicine. He loved arts and sciences, he was the patron of Vegerius, a jurist and a religious reformer, who also was his close councillor, and of the humanist Leonardo Bruno. He was buried in the Vatican Grottoes. His pontificate lasted about 2 years.

INNOCENT VII
1404 - 1406

205 – Born in Venice. Elected December 19, 1406 - died October 18, 1417. This was the worst period of the Western Schism. There were three different powers: Rome, Avignon, and Pisa. While the Schism was worsening, Emperor Sigismund called the 16th Ecumenical Council in Constance, which made a decision about the renunciation of the three rival Popes: Gregory XII, Benedict XIII and John XXIII. Gregory XII renounced the pontificate on July 4th 1415. At that time the anti-pope John XXIII shut himself up into the Vatican and linked that palace with Castel S. Angelo by means of a fortified corridor, the current "Passetto" was then called "the way to go". Apart from the conclave of Constance, all the other ones were held in Rome, except for the one concerning Pius VII, which took place in Venice. He was buried in the Cathedral of Recanati. His pontificate lasted 8 years and 7 months.

GREGORY XII
1406 - 1415

206 – Born in Rome. Elected November 21, 1417 - died February 20, 1431. He was a patron of the arts at the beginning of the Renaissance period. He celebrated the 5th Holy Year (1423) and for the first time a "Holy Door" was opened in the basilica of San Giovanni in Laterano. He also succeeded in re-obtaining all the territories of the church, fighting against brigandage. Martinus condemned again the heresy of Wycliff and Huss and did anything possible in order to save Joan of Arc from the stake. The Apostolic Secretariat was set up in the period of Martinus V (Secretariat of the Holy See after 1929 concordat), which was reformed definitively by Paul VI on August 15th 1967. He promulgated seven decrees among which the obligation for churchmen to wear a cassock which went to the heel. He was buried in San Giovanni in Laterano. His pontificate lasted 13 years and 3 months.

MARTINO V

1417   1431
ODDONE COLONNA

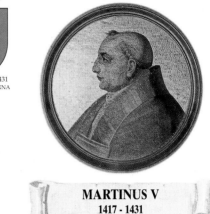

MARTINUS V
1417 - 1431

207 – Born in Venice. Elected March 11, 1431 - died February 23, 1447. He called the 17th Ecumenical Council in Basil, but later transferred to Ferrara and finally to Florence. Since he underscored the supremacy of the Pope over the Council, those who were opposed him elected the anti-pope Felix V; this was the last in history. Filarete produced the bronze central door of St. Peter's portico. Through the Pragmatic Sanction of Bourges, the supremacy of the Council over the Pope was reaffirmed. Eugene received an Ethiopian delegation sent by King David, who asked for the reunion of Copts and Catholics; in order to celebrate this event, Eugene donated St. Stephen's church to the Ethiopians, the building of which was ordered by St. Leo I (440-461) and called the church of the Abyssians. He was buried in the church of San Salvatore in Lauro. His pontificate lasted about 16 years.

EUGENIO IV

1431   1447
GABRIELE
CONDULMER

EUGENE IV
1431 - 1447

208 – Born in Sarzana. Elected March 19, 1447 - died March 24, 1455. After the election he did not choose a coat of arms and always used the crossed apostolic keys of St. Peter for his insignia. He signed a treaty with Frederick III of Austria to regulate the rights and the privileges of the Church and the Empire and in 1453 he crowned the Emperor in Rome. This was the last king to be crowned in St. Peter's. He politically reorganised France and England. He helped Spain to definitively expel the Saracens. He furthermore ordered the building of the current Basilica of St. Peter, in a position which is slightly different from that of the ancient Basilica of Constantine. Nicholas transferred all the ecclesiastical offices to the Vatican palaces and two Lateran libraries which were used to set up the Vatican Library. He celebrated the 6th Holy Year. He is buried in the Vatican Grottoes. His pontificate lasted 8 years.

NICCOLO V

1447   1455
TOMMASO
PARENTUCCELLI

NICHOLAS V
1447 - 1455

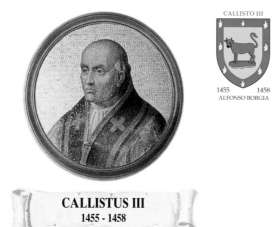

CALLISTUS III
1455 - 1458

209 – Born in Jativa (Spain). Elected August 20, 1455 - died August 6, 1458. He ordered to ring the bells every day at noon. He made Christianity flourish again in Sweden, Norway and Denmark. He introduced the Transfiguration Feast celebrated on August 6th. During his pontificate a big comet appeared in the sky, the famous "Haley" that reappeared again in 1910 and in 1996. He can be considered the founder of the Pontifical Navy (abolished on September 20th 1870). He armed a fleet at his expenses, with the contribution of cardinals, which crossed the Mediterranean and the Aegean Sea, causing many problems to Turkish ships. He rehabilitated the memory of Joan of Arc, who died on the stake and was considered an heretic and a witch, reaffirming her innocence. His mortal remains were transferred to the Spanish church of S. Maria di Monserrato in Rome. His pontificate lasted about 3 years and 4 months.

PIUS II
1458 - 1464

210 – Born in Siena. Elected September 13, 1458 - died August 15, 1464. In order to support the provinces oppressed by the Turks , he confirmed the alliance between the Kings of France, Burgundy, Hungary and Venice. He died while leaving for a holy war. He is considered founder of the Office of Fine Arts because he issued provisions for the protection and conservation of Roman and countryside monuments. He was a patron of the arts. He dreamt about the "perfect city", that is to say a city built following humanistic principles. He rebuilt Corsignano, his village of origin, nowadays called Pienza, according to Renaissance principles of Alberti and of the Vitruvius treaty "De Architettura", re-discovered in 1414: this is the rebuilding of the "ideal city" by Francesco Di Giorgio Martini preserved in Urbino. He canonized St. Catherine of Siena. He founded the College of Abbreviators, made up of scholars whose task was to collect, catalogue and correct all ecclesiastic documents. His body was transferred to the church of San Andrea della Valle. His pontificate lasted about 6 years.

PAUL II
1464 - 1471

211 – Born in Venice. Elected September 16, 1464 - died July 26, 1471. He decided that only cardinals could wear the red biretta. In order to ensure that each generation could benefit from forgiveness, he shortened the interval between Holy Years to 25 years; he also began to call them "Jubilee". He opposed the death penalty and did not allow its use during his pontificate. He provided his aid to the Albanian Giorgio Castrota, called Scanderberg, who committed himself in a terrible struggle against the Turks in order to free Albania; as you may know, Scanderberg is considered the national hero of Albania. He is buried in the Vatican Grottoes. His pontificate lasted about 7 years.

212 – Born in Savona. Elected August 25, 1471 - died August 12, 1484. He was a politician and a patron of the arts. He celebrated the 7th Jubilee in 1475, which lasted till Easter of 1476. He introduced the feast of St. Joseph celebrated on March 19th. He built the Sistine Chapel where Michelangelo painted his frescoes. The Swiss Guards, who still protect the Pope to this day, were set up during his pontificate. In 1471 some coins bearing the inscription "Urbe Restituta" were minted. Sixtus ordered the rebuilding of the so-called Ponte Rotto, built by Marcus Aurelius in 161 A.C. and collapsed in 792, who was therefore called "Ponte Sisto". Sixtus V put his personal collection of classical statues in his Roman palaces. This was the first museum of the world and the core of the current Capitoline Museums, originally opened to the public by Clement XII (1730-1740). He was buried in the Basilica of St. Peter. His pontificate lasted 13 years and 3 days.

SISTO IV

1471   1484
FRANCESCO
DELLA ROVERE

SIXTUS IV
1471 - 1484

213 – Born in Genoa. Elected September 12, 1484 - died July 25, 1492. He restored peace between the Catholic states. He fought against the trade of slaves and helped Christopher Columbus in his attempt to discover the Americas. Since he was suffering from stomach cancer, obviously the diagnosis is uncertain, he was very weak: his doctors thought about the possibility of injecting young blood in his veins, which were supposed to be rich in vital force: this was the first known attempt of making a transfusion. However, Innocent died soon afterwards on July 25th 1492, on the eve of the discovery of the Americas, for his doctors did not know anything about blood groups and RH factors. He was buried in the Basilica of St. Peter. His pontificate lasted 7 years and 10 months.

INNOCENZO VIII

1484   1492
GIOVANNI BATTISTA
CIBO

INNOCENT VIII
1484 - 1492

214 – Born in Jativa (Spain). Elected August 26. 1492 - died August 18, 1503. By splitting up the new lands of the Americas on the maps, he marked the fate of the new continent. He celebrated the 8th Jubilee (1500). He opened for the first time a Holy Door in St. Peter's, S. Paolo's and S. Maria Maggiore. The most beautiful work ordered by Alexander is the apartment Borgia in the Vatican, which was frescoed by Pinturicchio. He is buried in the Spanish church of Rome, S. Maria del Monserrato. His pontificate lasted 11 years.

ALESSANDRO VI

1492   1503
RODRIGO BORGIA

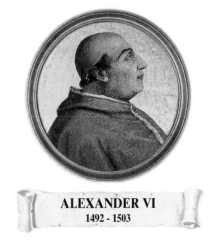

ALEXANDER VI
1492 - 1503

PIO III

1503   1503
FRANCESCO
TODESCHINI-PICCOLOMINI

215 – Born in Siena. Elected October 8, 1503 - died October 18, 1503. He accepted the elections after many pressures, because of his precarious state of health. During the crowning, his gout forced him to say Mass sitting down. He could not do much given the brevity of his pontificate, only 15 days. He was buried in San Andrea della Valle.

PIUS III
1503

GIULIO II

1503   1513
GIULIANO
DELLA ROVERE

216 – Born in Savona. Elected November 26, 1503 - died February 21, 1513. He fostered art and studies and made Rome become magnificent with the contribution provided by Raffaello and Michelangelo. He called the 18th Ecumenical Council. He completed the building of the Basilica of St. Peter, the biggest of the world. On April 18th 1506 he blessed and laid the foundation stone of the new St. Peter's, in a very deep hole dug where one of the 4 columns supporting the cupola was to be placed and also deposited in it an urn containing 12 coins among which two golden coins created for this event. He renewed the use of beard for popes, making it grow when he was already old. Before Julius we heard no news about the fact that the bodies of popes were opened and embalmed. Julius was the first: the last was Leo XIII. Julius institutionalised the Swiss Guards. The uniform with yellow and red stripes, (the colours of Rome) was designed by Michelangelo and was definitively adopted by Paul III in 1548. He was buried in the Basilica of St. Peter. His pontificate lasted about 9 years and 4 months.

JULIUS II
1503 - 1513

LEONE X

1513   1521
GIOVANNI
DE MEDICI

217 – Born in Florence. Elected March 19, 1513 - died December 1st 1521. He did not care about and did not know how to solve the serious schism caused by the former Augustinian monk Marin Luther, who married a former nun, Caterina Bora. He set up a censorship office concerning the printing of books, from which the Index was originated (the list of forbidden books to Catholics). He went ahead with the building of the new St. Peter's and made Raffaello paint the famous loggias in the Vatican. He was the founder of the Vatican Chapel of Cantors and was the creator and founder of the Institute of Antiquity and Fine Arts, having written a Breve about the conservation of the latter. He created the pawnshops and laws on pawn offices. He was buried in the Church of Santa Maria sopra Minerva. His pontificate lasted about 8 years and 9 months.

LEO X
1513 - 1521

218 – Born in Utrecht (Holland). Elected August 31, 1522 unknowingly while he was Bishop in Tortona - died September 14, 1523. He committed himself to struggle against those who opposed the Church and against the Turks, without being successful. Hadrian said that: "the Pope and the prelates must decorate churches, rather than decorate prelates with churches". He was the non-Italian Pope till current Pope John Paul II, the Polish Karol Wojtila. Since people used to say that Hadrian died as a consequence of too much drinking, Pasquinus, Roman talking statue, took revenge with a cutting remark: "Qui Iace Hadrian sesto, homo divino". He was buried in the Roman church of S. Maria dell'Anima. His pontificate lasted about 1 year and 8 months.

ADRIANO VI
1522 1523
ADRIANO FLORENSZ

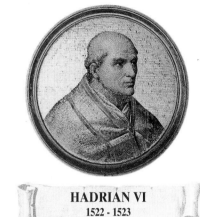

HADRIAN VI
1522 - 1523

219 – Born in Florence. Elected November 26, 1523 - died September 25, 1534. He did not succeed in settling disputes between the Catholics and the Lutheran reform; Charles V, who was Catholic, called a Diet in Spires, which condemned Lutheranism; however, the Lutheran princes, who wanted to take advantage of the assets of former convents, protested and were thereby defined "Protestants": the term was then used to define all the followers of Lutheranism. Given the majority of the latter, Charles V was forced to allow the new confession. Gustav Wasa, the king of Sweden, as well as the Norwegians and Danes took immediate advantage of this situation. Clement VII, like Hadrian VI, wanted to throw Pasquinus, a Roman talking statue, into the Tiber, but Torquato Tasso made him change his mind. During his pontificate, sacking and pestilence reduced the Roman population to 30,000 and Henry VIII, who had been excommunicated, rejected Christianity. He celebrated the 9th Jubilee. He was buried in S. Maria sopra Minerva. His pontificate lasted about 10 months.

CLEMENTE VII
1523 1534
GIULIO DE' MEDICI

CLEMENT VII
1523 - 1534

220 – Born in Rome. Elected November 3, 1534 - died November 10, 1549. He was a great patron of arts and culture; he appointed Michelangelo architect of St. Peter for life. In the framework of the Counter-Reformation he approved the Society of Jesus. He called the 19th Ecumenical Council. Through the Bull "Licet ab initio", dating back to July 21st 1542, Paul III founded the "Supreme Sacred Congregation of the Holy Office" to fight against heresy, crimes against Faith and the unity of the Church (apostasy, schisms, etc.). This office must not be confused with the Inquisition. These methods were renewed by Paul VI in 1965 with the "Sacred Congregation for the teaching of Faith". He issued the Bull for the announcement of the jubilee year in 1550 but he died before its opening. He was buried in the Basilica of St. Peter in one of the most beautiful sepulchres of the church. His pontificate lasted about 15 years and 1 month.

PAOLO III
1534 1549
ALESSANDRO FARNESE

PAUL III
1534 - 1549

221 – Born in Rome. Elected February 22, 1550 - died March 23, 1555. By reopening the Council of Trent he continued to oppose Lutheran theories. When Mary Tudor came to the throne of England, he sent a legate for the reintroduction of the catholic cult. He celebrated the 10th Jubilee Year (1550). In a Bull he established that two blood brothers could not be cardinals at the same time. The Protestant Reformation was increasingly counting on followers : it reached Scotland and vast areas of France; in this country, the Protestants were called Huguenots. Thanks to special faculties granted by Julius III, the first real university of Catholic studies was set up: it had already been founded by St. Ignatio of Loyola and St. Francis Borgia; enriched with donations and new buildings by Gregory XIII, it then took his name. He was buried in the Vatican Grottoes. His pontificate lasted 5 years and 1 month.

JULIUS III
1550 - 1555

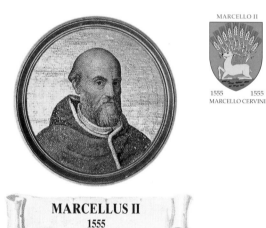

222 – Born in Montepulciano. Elected April 10, 1555 - died May 1st 1555. He was the last to maintain his Christian name. He endowed the curia with austerity and justice. He worried about the Russian and Mongolian peoples. Pierluigi of Palestrina composed the famous "Mass of Pope Marcellus". In this regard, it must be said that Marcellus II wanted to eliminate music from religious services, but Palestrina made him change his mind thanks to the composition of this Mass. The Pope, listening to the gravity of singing and the sweetness of music, did not allow for music, but also had this genre of music played in his Chapel. His pontificate lasted only 22 days. He is buried in the Vatican Grottoes.

MARCELLUS II
1555

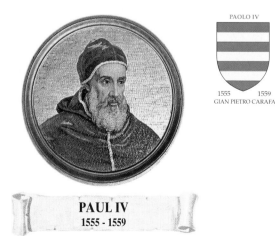

223 – Born in Naples. Elected May 26, 1555 - died August 18, 1559. He promoted the reformation of customs. He fought against the Inquisition and Lutheran heresy. He forced the Jews to live in the "Ghetto". Paul IV brought to light the idea of a Vatican Typography, the "Printing-office of the Roman people". He was the first Pope to use the palanquin from the Vatican to San Giovanni. He wrote a Bull in which he threatened with the death penalty every man that depended economically on a woman as well as any woman who accepted this situation. He was buried in S. Maria sopra Minerva. His pontificate lasted 4 years and 3 months.

PAUL IV
1555 - 1559

224 – Born in Milan. Elected January 1st 1560 - died December 9, 1565. He reconvoked and concluded the Council of Trent. He took action to ensure that Emanuele Filiberto was given back the territory of Piedmont, thereby making the Savoys a part of history. He forgave all the guilty. He consecrated Cardinal St. Charles Borromeo and appointed him Secretary of State, this is the first time that this office appears in the Pontifical State. Pius IV donated the Palace of St. Mark, built upon request of Paul II, to the Republic of Venice as a symbol of gratitude for having allowed the development of the Council of Trent and to give the Republic a distinguished site for its Embassy. From 1925 to 1943 this palace was used by Benito Mussolini as his personal office when he was leader of the Fascist government. He was buried in S. Maria degli Angeli, according to his will. His pontificate lasted about 6 years.

PIO IV

1560   1565
GIOVAN ANGELO
DE MEDICI

PIUS IV
1560 - 1565

225 – Born in Bosco. Elected January 17, 1566 - died May 1st 1572. In order to stem heresy, he promoted education among the people. He excommunicated Elizabeth of England. He was the author of Lepanto's Christian victory against the Saracens. He ordered the use of the Roman Missal, following the decisions taken in Trent, although the churches which had a different tradition for at least two hundred years were exempted. A typical example is the Ambrosian Missal of Milan, which is quite different from the Roman one, especially in terms of its texts and chronology. Another church having its own rites is the Spanish Church of Toledo. He is buried in S. Maria Maggiore, in the chapel of the Holy Crib. His pontificate lasted about 6 years and 4 months.

S. PIO. V.

1566   1572
ANTONIO (MICHELE)
GHISLIERI

PIUS V, ST
1566 - 1572

226 – Born in Bologna. Elected May 25, 1572 - died April 10, 1585. He opened seminars in Vienna, Prague, Graz and Japan. He celebrated the 11th Jubilee Year (1575). He reformed the calendar for the whole world and suddenly October 4th became October 15th, the days left were eliminated. As soon as he was elected, he abolished the habit of holding an expensive banquet for cardinals and ambassadors on the occasion of a crowning, as well as that of throwing money to the people. Gregory ordered the building of the Torre dei Venti, which represented the first section of the Vatican astronomical observatory, one of the first in the world; two further towers were later added to this structure in the papal gardens. The Observatory was moved to Castel Gandolfo in 1933 He was buried in the Basilica of St. Peter at his own expense. His pontificate lasted 12 years and 11 months.

GREGORIO XIII

1572   1585
UGO BONCOMPAGNI

GREGORY XIII
1572 - 1585

227 – Born in Grottammare. Elected May 1st 1585 - died August 27, 1590. He resumed the already begun reformation of the Church and was very strict. He completed the works of the Cupola of St. Peter and the obelisk on the square. Sixtus V was the Pope of the obelisks; he ordered the construction of four obelisks in Piazza S. Pietro, Piazza dell'Esquilino, Piazza del Popolo and Piazza del Quirinale. The building of the obelisk in St. Peter's square, by the architect Domenico Fontana, lead to the legend of the famous "water for the ropes". He commissioned the richly decorated palace that contains the Holy Stairs, which is said to have been in Pilate's praetorial. He chose the name Sixtus and was the last Pope bearing this name. He regulated the issue of the Patron Saint: only one for each town, to be elected by the people and the local clergy. He was the first Pope to die in the Quirinale Palace. He was buried in the Chapel of the Holy Crib in S. Maria Maggiore. His pontificate lasted 5 years and 4 months.

SIXTUS V
1585 - 1590

228 – Born in Rome. Elected September 15, 1590 - died September 27, 1590. He had a good and merciful character. He wanted to base his government on the Trent decrees but was affected by malaria. He left all his fortune to charity. He died after 13 days of pontificate. He ordered to cover the nakedness of the statue of the Truth on Paul III's sepulchre in St. Peter's. He was buried in the Church of S. Maria sopra Minerva.

URBAN VII
1590

229 – Born in Cremona. Elected December 8, 1590 - died October 1591. He was a strict man, with an ascetic nature, who was cheated by his inefficient councillors. He confirmed the right to asylum in the Embassies of the Holy See. He excommunicated Henry IV who co-operated with the reformists and then abjured. He excommunicated Henry IV of Navarra who in order to obtain the throne of France, declared: "Paris is well worth a Mass!". He was buried in the Basilica of St. Peter. His pontificate lasted only 10 months.

GREGORY XIV
1590 - 1591

230 – Born in Bologna. Elected November 3, 1591 - died suddenly on December 30, 1591. He helplessly witnessed a terrible epidemic of pestilence but fought successfully against brigandage and various internal factions. He favoured Philip II of Spain and the Alliance against Henry IV, encouraging Alexander Farnese to go to France to free the city of Rouen. Innocent died only two months after his election. He is buried in the Vatican Grottoes.

INNOCENZO IX

1591   1591
GIOVANNI ANTONIO
FACCHINETTI

INNOCENT IX
1591

231 – Born in Florence. Elected February 9, 1592 - died March 3, 1605. He succeeded in restoring peace between France and Spain. He celebrated the 12th Jubilee Year (1600) and defined the "Forty hours". Maderno sculpted St. Cecily, the patron of Music, according to the image he had of her when he visited her sepulchre for the first time. He was the first Pope who left from the Quirinale, instead of the Vatican, to reach the Basilica of San Giovanni in Laterano. The custom of sending blessed swaddling clothes to new born sovereigns dates back to this period. He died suddenly while he was participating in a session of the Court of the Inquisition. In order to pay his respects to the Council of Trent, he ordered that the book "Pontificale Romanum", which deals with the celebration of Sacraments, Consecrations and blessings, become the official text of the Church, . He was buried in S. Maria Maggiore. His pontificate lasted 13 years and 1 month.

CLEMENTE VIII

1592   1605
IPPOLITO
ALDOBRANDINI

CLEMENT VIII
1592 - 1605

232 – Born in Florence. Elected April 10, 1605 - died April 27, of the same year. He devoted himself to an ascetic life and was very popular for his generosity. While riding to the Lateran, to take possession of the Episcopal Seat, he did not feel well and died. Immediately afterwards people said he died from poisoning after having smelled a rose. Today, the bushes of roses sculpted by Algardi on the funeral urn of Pope Leo XI continue to remind us of this suspect. He died after only 26 days of pontificate. He is buried in the Basilica of St. Peter.

LEONE XI

1605   1605
ALESSANDRO
DE MEDICI

LEO XI
1605

233 – Born in Rome. Elected May 29, 1605 - died January 28, 1621. He had relations with Michael Romanoff of Russia and asked for the help of civilised nations to stop the prosecution of Christians in Japan and China. He was in favour of astronomy but he let Copernicus be condemned. He cared about Roman waters and fountains and reactivated the ancient aqueduct, which brought water from Bracciano lake to Trastevere, dating back to the period of Emperor Trajan. He ordered that priests must have a book containing the names of the baptised, the confirmed, the married and the state of souls. Paul V was the first to introduce the agricultural credit, with "motuproprio" dated October 19th 1611. He beatified S. Filippo Neri and Ignazio of Loyola and canonized Francesca Romana and Carlo Borromeo. He introduced the Office of St. Casimiro into the Breviary. He established the feast of Sts. Guardian Angels. He was a great patron of the arts. Among his protected, it is worth mentioning Guido Reni, who was granted the privilege of keeping his hat on in presence of the Pope. He is buried in S. Maria Maggiore. His pontificate lasted about 15 years and 8 months.

PAUL V
1605 - 1621

234 – Born in Bologna. Elected February 14, 1621 - died July 8, 1623. During his brief pontificate, he encouraged Irish people and favoured the Catholic re-establishment in France. He cared about missions for which he set up the Congregation of "Propaganda fide". The famous Heidelberg Library, which is now called the Palatine Library, was donated to him by Maximilian of Bavaria. Gregory is responsible for the definitive legislation of the conclave, which was used till the election of John Paul I in 1978. Later Paul VI, adapted it in order to make it more flexible to current times and with the Bull "Aeterni Patris Filius", he reaffirmed, among other things, the secrecy of the conclave. He is buried in the Roman church of San Ignazio. His pontificate lasted 2 years and 5 months.

GREGORY XV
1621 - 1623

235 – Born in Florence. Elected September 29, 1623 - died July 29, 1644. He worked on Holy Texts: Pontifical, Breviary, Ritual, Martyrology. When he was condemned, Galileo said "and yet it moves". He celebrated the 13th Jubilee Year (1625). He had his summer residence built in Castel Gandolfo (Rome). During the Consistory held on June 10th 1630, Urban VIII ordered that the cardinals had to be addressed using the words "His Eminence" instead of "distinguished". He ordered the restoration of the Pantheon and took about 150,000 kilos of bronze from the bronze trussing of its portico to build the wonderful spiral columns of the baldachin of the papal altar in St. Peter's, made by Bernini, as well as for the cannons at Castel S. Angelo. He is buried in the Basilica of St. Peter. His pontificate was very long: 20 years and 11 months.

URBAN VIII
1623 - 1644

236 – Born in Rome. Elected October 4, 1644 - died January 1st 1655. He recommended the enfranchisement of serfs to Alex I, Czar of Russia. He disapproved of the Treaty of Westfalen since many cities were then governed by Protestants. He celebrated the 14th Jubilee Year (1650). On his election day, the cupola of St. Peter's was lit up for the first time. He ordered Bernini to build the Fountain of the Four Rivers in Piazza Navona, which later became extremely popular. He ordered that the Cardinals had to be called only Eminence and that their emblem was to be the cardinal cap. He was buried in the church of S. Agnese. His pontificate lasted about 10 years and 4 months.

INNOCENZO X

1644　　　1655
GIOVANNI BATTISTA
PAMPHILJ

INNOCENT X
1644 - 1655

237 – Born in Siena. Elected April 18, 1655 - died May 22, 1667. He tried to stem the dissemination of Protestantism in Italy and in England. He completed the restoration works for St. Peter's square, with the Colonnade by Bernini and the two fountains. He cordially received Queen Christine of Sweden, hosting her in the Vatican and, on Christmas night, he confirmed her. He added valuable collections to the Vatican Library and set up a secret archive. In order to remind himself that he would have to die one day, he kept a coffin under his bed and drank from a silver cup with an image of death on the bottom. Convinced about his doctrinal positions, he condemned once again the Five Propositions by Jansen. He was buried in the Basilica of St. Peter. His pontificate lasted 12 years and 1 month.

ALESSANDRO VII

1655　　　1667
FABIO CHIGI

ALEXANDER VII
1655 - 1667

238 – Born in Pistoia. Elected June 26, 1667 - died December 9, 1669. He acted as a mediator in the succession wars that took place in France, Spain, England and Holland and ended with the Peace of Aachen, called Clementina. The colonnade of St. Peter's was decorated with the statues of 140 saints. At the request of Pope Clement IX, Bernini did the decorations of Ponte Elio (S. Angelo) with the magnificent angels, soaring over the "blond river". He established a new relationship with the faithful, which recalls the one recently adopted by John XXIII; he personally confessed the penitents . He was buried in Santa Maria Maggiore. His pontificate lasted about 2 years and 5 months.

CLEMENTE IX

1667　　　1669
GIULIO ROSPIGLIOSI

CLEMENT IX
1667 - 1669

1669   1676
EMILIO ALTIERI

239 – Born in Rome. Elected May 11, 1669 - died July 22, 1676. He took part in the election of the King of Poland, favouring the appointment of John Sobieski, who was preferred given his Christian faith and the success he recorded against the Turks in the battle of Chaezim. He celebrated the 15th Jubilee Year (1675). He was elected after 5 months of discussions of the conclave. He had a harsh dispute with France with regard to the problem of the right to regalia, which was confirmed by Louis XIV. He was buried in the Basilica of St. Peter. His pontificate lasted about 6 years and 3 months.

CLEMENT X
1669 - 1676

B. INNOCENZO XI

1676   1689
BENEDETTO
ODESCALCHI

240 – Born in Como. Elected October 4, 1676 - died August 12, 1689. He abolished the right to immunity and defeated nepotism. He was opposed to the arrogance of Louis XIV of France. He pushed the Polish King Sobieskj to defeat the Turks in Vienna. He introduced the celebration of the Saint name of Mary on September 12th. Since he was reluctant to give his approvals, he was defined "Papa Minga". He ordered that women had to go to church wearing modest clothes and with their heads covered. Innocent XI was the first Pope to grant indulgences to those who exercised the XIV stations, which were adopted and recognised only at the end of the 17th Century. The first representation of the scenes of the Passion are attributed to Alvaro the Blessed in 1620, a Dominican monk who returned to his convent in Cordova after having been in the Holy Land. He was buried in the Basilica of St. Peter. His pontificate lasted about 12 years and 11 months.

INNOCENT XI, BL.
1676 - 1689

ALESSANDRO VIII

1689   1691
PIERO OTTOBONI

241 – Born in Venice. Elected October 16, 1689 - died February 2, 1691. He was appointed thanks to the influence of Louis of France, who came to an agreement on the 4 propositions of the "Gallican liberties". He provided aid to the King of Poland and the people of Venice in a fight against the Turks. He enlarged the Vatican library by buying, at his own expense, the library of Queen Christine of Sweden. He reduced the charge for grinding by a "paolo" and, in return, his citizens minted two coins bearing the inscription: "Re frumentaria restituta". His pontificate lasted 1 year and 4 months.

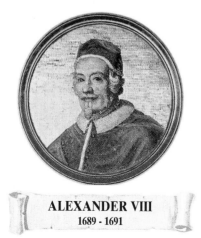

ALEXANDER VIII
1689 - 1691

242 – Born in Naples. Elected July 15, 1691 - died September 27, 1700. He forced priests to wear a cassock and to do spiritual exercises everyday. Louis XIV renounced the "Gallican propositions" and the Pope recognised the Bishops of the King. He called the 16th Jubilee (1700). He supported the missions to Asia, America and Africa. Thanks to the success recorded by Prince Eugene of Savoy in Zentha against Mustafa, Innocent XII could witness the restoration of peace between Austria and Turkey, which marked the fall of the Turks. In Ripa Grande, he set up the St. Michael Nursery Home for the vocational training of youths; today, this building is the site of the Ministry of Cultural Heritage. He was buried in a very unpretentious sarcophagus, ordered by himself. His pontificate lasted about 9 years and 3 months.

INNOCENZO XII

1691   1700
ANTONIO PIGNATELLI

INNOCENT XII
1691 - 1700

243 – Born in Urbino. Elected December 8, 1700 - died March 19, 1721. After having heard the news about his election, he accepted after 7 days to be absolutely certain of his eligibility. Learned and keen to the arts, he enriched the Vatican Library with ancient eastern codes. He concluded the 16th Jubilee Year (1700). He founded the Church in the Philippine Islands and sent missionaries to China, Persia and India. He was the last Pope to have a beard or goatee. In the Bull "unigenitus" (1713) he reaffirmed that the Jansenists were to be considered heretics. He was the first one to order that no work of art was to be taken away from Rome, therefore establishing the first legislation to protect its artistic heritage. He created an Academy of painting and sculpture at the Campidoglio. He was keen about archaeology, which began to have its first scientific followers in this period. He was buried under the pavement of the Choir Section in St. Peter's. His pontificate was one of the longest lasting 21 years and 3 months.

CLEMENTE XI

1700   1721
GIAN FRANCESCO
ALBANI

CLEMENT XI
1700 - 1721

244 – Born in Rome. Elected May 18, 1721 - died March 7, 1724. He reconfirmed the Bull "Unigenitus" to the French clergy who had not accepted it. He firmly took action in the Spanish Church, which wanted to ignore the authority of Rome, even if not officially. He started the definitive restoration of San Giovanni in Laterano's facade. He sent 100,000 scudos to the Knights of Malta to support their fight against Islam. Like his predecessor Clement XI, he legalised the lotto game in the State. He is buried in the Vatican Grottoes. His pontificate lasted about 2 years and 10 months.

INNOCENZO XIII

1721   1724
MICHELANGELO
DEI CONTI

INNOCENT XIII
1721 - 1724

BENEDETTO XIII

1724   1730
PIETRO FRANCESCO
ORSINI

245 – Born at Gravina in Puglia. Elected May 4, 1724 - died March 2, 1730. He concentrated, above all, on spiritual teachings. On the occasion of the 17th Jubilee Year he inaugurated the wonderful staircase at Trinita dei Monti in Rome. He canonized St. Louis Gonzaga and St. Stanislaus, patron of Poland. He forbade churchmen to wear wigs and this decision was reluctantly accepted by Cardinal Bentivoglio and Cardinal Alberoni, since they used to wear it for reasons regarding their health. He renewed the announcements already issued by Innocent XII in 1696 for the lotto game to all Roman citizens and its province. He was buried in S. Maria sopra Minerva. His pontificate lasted about 5 years and 9 months.

BENEDICT XIII
1724 - 1730

CLEMENTE XII

1730   1740
LORENZO CORSINI

246 – Born in Florence. Elected July 16, 1730 - died February 2, 1740. He did not interfere in the numerous wars that broke out in that period. He abolished the ban regarding the lotto, because of the adverse balance of the Pontifical State. The drawing used to take place in the loggias of the Campidoglio and the first numbers were: 56-11-54-18-6. He founded an institute for Chinese youth in Naples. He excommunicated the Masonic institutions. Clement XII was the author of the current system of paving-stones, which are typical of Roman streets. He had the streets of Rome paved with squared stones and enlarged, levelled and straightened out part of Via del Corso. He opened the Capitoline Museums to the public, and enriched them with new works. He is buried in the Basilica of San Giovanni in Laterano. His pontificate lasted about 9 years and 6 months.

CLEMENT XII
1730 - 1740

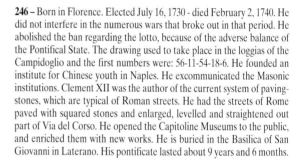

BENEDETTO XIV

1740   1758
PROSPERO
LAMBERTINI

247 – Born in Bologna. Elected August 22, 1740 - died May 3, 1758. He was the most learned Pope of his century. Together with St. Leonard, he spread the word about the devotion of the "Via Crucis" and celebrated the 18th Jubilee Year (1750). He ordered the continuation of the Papal portraits in the Basilica of San Paolo in Rome. On the occasion of a solemn religious service, he defined the Coliseum as a public church. He defended marriage and prohibited duels. He also abolished the Select Knights corps, which was responsible for the pope's safety. He published a magnificent work on the beatification and canonisation of saints. The current Canonical Code was based, to a large extent, upon the so-called Bollarium Benedicti XIV. He founded the Holy or Christian Museum in the Vatican and the Capitoline picture gallery. He is buried in the Basilica of St. Peter. His pontificate lasted about 17 years and 9 months.

BENEDICT XIV
1740 - 1758

248 – Born in Venice. Elected July 16, 1758 - died mysteriously February 2, 1769. His pontificate had to cope with the "Enlightenment". Austere, even if faithful to a conservatory attitude, he was not liked by many Catholic states where many secular rights of the church were abolished. The most difficult issue he had to tackle was that concerning the Jesuits, who had to face the opposition of the entire Catholic world; the Pope uselessly issued many bulls to defend them. Clement XIII tried to drain the Pontine marshes, a project which Sixtus V had already thought about, and completed the building of the Fontana di Trevi, one of the most beautiful baroque monuments. He was buried in the Basilica of St. Peter. His pontificate lasted about 10 years and 5 months.

CLEMENTE XIII

1758   1769
CARLO REZZONICO

CLEMENT XIII
1758 - 1769

249 – Born in Sant'Arcangelo (Rimini). Elected June 4, 1769 - supposedly died from poisoning on September 22, 1774. He tried to resume normal relations with Catholic countries. He founded the museum of epigraphs called Clementino. He modified the regulation of the Sistine Choir. Clement XIV had foreseen the end of temporal power and consequently wrote to a friend: "The Holy See will not decay since it is the core and the centre of unity, but the Popes will be forced to give back everything they have received". Despite the numerous attempts to settle disputes, on July 21st 1773 he finally promulgated the "Breve" for the abolishment of the "Dominus ac Redemtior". The Jesuits, chased away from the Americas, looked for shelter in two non-catholic states, Russia and Prussia, and remained there till the reorganisation of the Order (Pius VII - 251). He continued the works for the drainage of the Pontine marshes, the construction of the foundation for the Fiumicino quarter and the building of the foundation for the Clementino Museum in the Vatican. He was buried in the Roman church of the SS. Apostoli. His pontificate lasted about 5 years and 4 months.

CLEMENTE XIV

1769   1774
VINCENZO ANTONIO
GANGANELLI

CLEMENT XIV
1769 - 1774

250 – Born in Cesena. Elected February 22, 1775 - died February 29, 1799. He celebrated the 19th Jubilee Year (1775). Forced to interrupt relations with France, he was forced to pay them a lot of money and give them many works of art. Napoleon conquered Rome and arrested the Pope. He ordered the casting of the 2-meter-wide bells of St. Peter's. Night lighting and the street-lamps were first introduce to Rome, during the pontificate of Pius VI. He was the last Pope to ride a horse during the procession towards the Basilica of San Giovanni in Laterano as bishop of Rome. When he was a cardinal, he used to wear a wig, but after the election he presented himself with his own hair: he did this because no Pope had ever worn a wig. He is buried in the Basilica of St. Peter. His pontificate lasted 24 years and a half and was one of the longest.

PIO VI

1775   1799
GIOVANNI ANGELO
BRASCHI

PIUS VI
1775 - 1799

PIO VII

1800   1823
BARNABA
CHIARAMONTI

251 – Born in Cesena. Elected March 21, 1800 - died July 20, 1823. Following Napoleon's will, he obtained the Concordat that restored the Church power in France. He crowned Napoleon in Paris, but after a series of disputes he excommunicated him. He introduced the white and yellow pontifical flag. On August 7, 1814, he published the Bull "sollecitudo animarum", through which he rehabilitated the Jesuits; subsequently, he reintroduced the Holy Office, abolished by Napoleon. He founded the lapidarian gallery in the Vatican, the result of very patient work carried out by Gaetano Marini, and the Chiaromonti Museum. Above all, he founded the Vatican Picture gallery, one of the richest in the world. He is buried in the Basilica of St. Peter. His pontificate lasted 23 years and 5 months.

PIUS VII
1800 - 1823

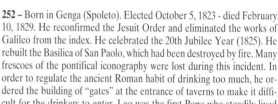

LEONE XII

1823   1829
ANNIBALE DELLA
GENGA

252 – Born in Genga (Spoleto). Elected October 5, 1823 - died February 10, 1829. He reconfirmed the Jesuit Order and eliminated the works of Galileo from the index. He celebrated the 20th Jubilee Year (1825). He rebuilt the Basilica of San Paolo, which had been destroyed by fire. Many frescoes of the pontifical iconography were lost during this incident. In order to regulate the ancient Roman habit of drinking too much, he ordered the building of "gates" at the entrance of taverns to make it difficult for the drinkers to enter. Leo was the first Pope who steadily lived in the Vatican, rather than in the Quirinale. He is buried in the Basilica of St. Peter. His pontificate lasted about 5 years and 5 months.

LEO XII
1823 - 1829

PIO VIII

1829   1830
FRANCESCO SAVERIO
CASTIGLIONI

253 – Born in Cingoli. Elected April 5, 1829 - died November 30, 1830. The riots of the Risorgimento were gaining ground in Italy. He was open-minded and negotiated with the Sultan in favour of the Armenians. He introduced the postal service of the Vatican State. He intensified missions all over the world. The people of Rome were immediately in favour of Pope Pius VIII because he ordered the abolishment of the detested "gates" in front of taverns, introduced by Leo XII. He fostered the development of agriculture as well as that of the Post Offices as a regular and constant service provided by the State. He died after 1 year and 8 months of pontificate. He is buried in the Basilica of St. Peter.

PIUS VIII
1829 - 1830

254 – Born in Belluno. Elected February 6, 1831 - died June 1st 1846. He counted on the powers of the Holy Alliance (Austria, Prussia and Russia) to govern the Pontifical States. He modified the full age from 25 to 21 years. He founded the Egyptian and Etruscan Museum. He was a good church governor and he was open-minded enough to abolish the public lists of citizens who had not respected the Easter duty and give more living space to the Jews living in the Ghetto. He ordered the rectification of the Aniene, the straightening of the mouth of the Tiber and the restructuring of the port of Civitavecchia. He completed and consecrated (1834) the Roman cemetery of Verano, which contains many monuments. He is buried in the Basilica of St. Peter. His pontificate lasted about 15 years and 4 months.

GREGORIO XVI

1831 1846
BARTOLOMEO ALBERTO
CAPPELLARI

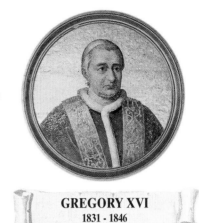

GREGORY XVI
1831 - 1846

255 – Giovanni Maria Mastai-Ferretti, born in Senigallia. Elected June 21, 1846 - died February 2, 1878. He celebrated the 21st Jubilee Year (1875) without opening the Holy doors and he established the infallibility of the Pope when speaking ex cattedra. On September 20th 1870, Rome became the capital of the Kingdom of Italy. The feast of the Immaculate Conception (on December 8th) has its origins in the Byzantine rite celebrated in the VIII century. Sixtus VI approved it definitively with the Bull "Prae excelsa" on March 1st 1476; Pius IX proclaimed it an obligatory Holy Day. He called an Ecumenical Council, the 1st Vatican Council. The Pope never forgot his pastoral role. On January 9th 1878, when he was informed about the fact that Vittorio Emanuele was on the point of death, he lifted the interdict and gave him his blessing; when the king died, he simply commented: "poor man, not only did he want to take my states here on earth, but he also wants to take my place in heaven!". Soon afterwards, Pius IX died on February 7th 1878. He died at the age of 86 after 31 years of pontificate, the longest recorded so far. He is buried in San Lorenzo al Verano. Pius IX was the last Pope-king: the temporal power of the Catholic Church had lasted for 1115 years, since the election of Pope Stephen III.

PIO IX

1846 1878
GIOVANNI M.
MASTAI FERRETTI

PIUS IX
1846 - 1878

256 – Gioacchino Pecci, born in Carpineto. Elected March 3, 1878 - died July 20, 1903. He published the encyclical "Rerum Novarum" concerning labour and social policy. He was the first Pope to be filmed. He celebrated the 22nd Jubilee Year and St. Peter's was lit for the first time using electricity. He allowed the scholars to have access to the Vatican Archives. He enriched the Vatican library with the Visconti library and the Borghese codes. Leo XIII introduced telephones and radiators in the Vatican but never accepted the use of a car. Leo XIII regulated the use of the "zucchetto"; a small circular skull-cap to be worn by Popes, cardinals, bishops and prelates. It is made of silk cloth, only the Pope's is made of velvet; it is violet for bishops; red for cardinals, white for the Pope and black for all other prelates. The zucchetto is also called "Soli Deo" since it must be taken off only during the bow to the Holy Sacrament. He died at the age of 93. His body was transferred to San Giovanni in Laterano. His pontificate lasted 25 years and 5 months.

LEONE XIII

1878 1903
GIOACCHINO PECCI

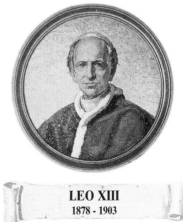

LEO XIII
1878 - 1903

257 – Giuseppe Sarto, born in Riese. Elected August 9, 1903 - died August 20, 1914. He terminated the "Codification of Canonical Law". He started the publication of the "Acta Apostolicae Sedis", which reports the laws and documents of the unabridged edition. He introduced the elevation of the Host and the chalice. He reorganised the Observatory and the Vatican Picture Gallery and founded the Biblical Institute. As to the Kingdom of Italy, he lifted the veto concerning the participation of Catholics in public life. Another important work done by the Pope is represented by the reforms of the Missal, the Breviary and the sacred music, with regard to which he co-operated with Lorenzo Perosi. He is buried in St. Peter's altar of the Presentation. On May 29th 1954 he was canonized by Pius XII. His pontificate lasted about 11 years.

PIUS X, ST.
1903 - 1914

BENEDETTO XV

1914   1922
GIACOMO
DELLA CHIESA

258 – Francesco Della Chiesa, born in Genoa. Elected September 6, 1914 - died January 22, 1922. The States which had a diplomatic site in the Vatican became 27 instead of 14, including England which had abolished it three centuries before. He beatified Joan of Arc and founded the University of the Sacro Cuore. He resumed diplomatic relations with England and France and by means of the Encyclical published on May 23rd 1920 he established a new protocol for the visits of Catholic Sovereigns to Rome. He confirmed the condemnation of "modernism" expressed by Pius X. In 1917, he published the Code of Canonical Law, started in conformity with Pius X's will. He approved the project of a Museum devoted to St. Peter, made with the collection of all the remains found in the old Constantinian Basilica. He lifted the veto concerning the visits of Catholic foreign sovereigns to the King of Italy. He was buried in the Vatican Grottoes. His pontificate lasted 7 years and a half.

BENEDICT XV
1914 - 1922

PIO XI

1922   1939
ACHILLE RATTI

259 – Achille Ratti, born in Desio. Elected February 12, 1922 - died February 10, 1939. On February 11th 1929 he signed together with Benito Mussolini the Concordat between the Church and the Italian state. On the occasion of the XIX Centenary of the Redemption (1933) he celebrated a Holy Year. G. Marconi built the Vatican Radio. His first words after having accepted the election were "...I want my first blessing to be a sign of peace and I will give it from the balcony of St. Peter's"; this exceptional event had not occurred since 1870 when Rome became part of the Kingdom of Italy. He set up the "Russicum". He established the missionary Museum in the Lateran, the Athenaeum of Propaganda Fide. Devised and built by Guglielmo Marconi, on February 12th 1931 Pius XI inaugurated the first and the biggest radio short-wave transmitter in the world. The first message read by the Pope ended with the same words of the Holy Scripture: "Listen, oh Heavens...listen oh land..listen, people of the world..". He died on February 10th, on the eve of the anniversary of the Conciliation. His pontificate lasted 17 years.

PIUS XI
1922 - 1939

260 – Eugenio Pacelli, born in Rome. Elected March 2, 1939, on the day of his 63rd birthday. He died October 9, 1958. He fought against the prosecution of Marxism. During the excavations below the Basilica, the Sepulchre of St. Peter was discovered. He celebrated the 24th Jubilee Year (1950) and proclaimed the Dogma of the Assumption of the Virgin Mary, which gave origin to the custom of blessing the statue of the Virgin Mary in Piazza di Spagna on December 8th. During his pontificate, Pius XII never left Rome or Castel Gandolfo, his summer residence. His longest journey was to Santa Maria di Galeria, on October 27th 1957, to inaugurate the new Vatican Radio Station (more than 1,000 KW of power): this town is 27 kilometres from Rome. He is buried in the Vatican Grottoes. His pontificate lasted about 18 and a half years.

PIO XII

1939   1958
EUGENIO PACELLI

PIUS XII
1939 - 1958

261 – Angelo Giuseppe Roncalli, born at Sotto il Monte (Bergamo). Elected October 28, 1958 - died June 3, 1963. With his Bull "Humanae salutis" he called the 21st Ecumenical Council Vatican II (October 11th 1962). The subject of the council was: liturgical life and social relationships, the Church and the modern world. His beatification is under way. The new Pope, endowed with a good and simple looking attitude, as opposed to the detached and ascetic Pius XII, revealed himself immediately as a Pope of transition and balance between the two different trends of traditionalists and the supporters of a greater opening of the Church. Soon after the consecration, which took place on November 4th, he began to visit parishes, hospitals and jails. Even during his pontificate, John XXIII continued to shock the conservatives when he received the son-in-law of Kruschev, the Russian Head of State, therefore ignoring the excommunication launched to the communists by Pope Pacelli. John raised the number of cardinals to 75, instead of the 70 previously established by Sixtus V. He also ordered the revision of the list of saints, which underwent a careful critical control. The death of John XXIII caused great emotion all over the world. He was buried in the Vatican Grottoes. His pontificate lasted 4 years and 8 months.

GIOVANNI XXIII

1958   1963
ANGELO GIUSEPPE
RONCALLI

JOHN XXIII
1958 - 1963

262 – Giovanni B. Montini, born in Concesio (Brescia). Elected June 21, 1963 - died August 6, 1978. He concluded the Vatican II Council (December 8th 1965). He celebrated the 25th Jubilee Year (1975). He was the first Pope to leave Europe. He allowed the clergy the use of a suit. He created the "Episcopal Synod". Paul VI established that the Mass had to be said in the mother language of the country and not in Latin - except for solemn ceremonies. He gave the new form of mensa to the altar, which in new churches had to be placed towards the faithful and at the actual centre of the building. Pope Montini aimed for the reform and the internationalisation of the Curia, the enlargement of the Sacred College from 103 to 120 members and the participation of cardinals from the third world. He wrote a letter to the members of the "Red Brigades" in which he begged for the liberation of Aldo Moro, president of the Christian Democrats, who was condemned to death by them. He ordered the building of the famous Sala Nervi, which bears the name of the architect that projected it, to be used during papal hearings held on Wednesdays. He renewed the legislation concerning the conclave and the Vacancy of the See. He was buried in the Vatican Grottoes. His pontificate lasted about 15 years and 2 months.

PAOLO VI

1963   1978
GIOVANNI BATTISTA
MONTINI

PAUL VI
1963 - 1978

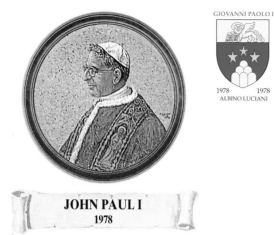

GIOVANNI PAOLO I

1978   1978
ALBINO LUCIANI

JOHN PAUL I
1978

263 – Albino Luciani, born in Forni di Canale (Belluno). Elected August 26,1978 - died September 28, 1978. Pope Luciani was the first Pope in history to name himself with a double name. On his very first Urbi et Orbi blessing from the balcony of St. Peter's, in a brief message he explained that the two names referred to his two predecessors to whom he felt very obliged. He refused the use of the gestatorial chair, the Tiara and did not want to be crowned. He died of heart failure while reading in bed. The announcement of his death to the world said: "This morning, September 29, 1978, the Pope's private secretary, as he usually did, went to look for him in his private chapel, since the Pope was not there the secretary went to his room and found him dead in bed, with the lights still on, as if he was reading". His pontificate was very brief: only 33 days. He is remembered as the smiling Pope. He is buried in the Vatican Grottoes.

GIOVANNI PAOLO II

1978
KAROL WOITYLA

JOHN PAUL II
1978 -

264 – Karol Wojtyla born at Wodivic in Poland. He is the first Pontiff of Polish origin and the first non-Italian Pope after 455 years, since Hadrian VI. Theologian, writer and poet, he is a Pope with an itinerant apostolate. Including his historic visit to Cuba, he has travelled internationally visiting 100 countries, including those without a catholic majority. He has been invited twice, February 3, 1979 and April 10, 1995, to give a speech at the UN. He has spoken to the Seats of major World Institutions, i.e. UNESCO, FAO and the European Parliament. In 1979, he went to Constantinople to meet with the orthodox patriarch Demetrio I. After a millennial separation, he reconciled with the Jewish community, on April 13, 1986, with a visit to Rome's Synagogue where he prayed with the "older brothers" and embraced the rabbi. On January 1, 1986, he went to Assisi to pray for peace together with the representatives of different religious doctrines from around the world. There was an attempt on his life during a general audience in St. Peter's Square on May 13, 1981. He has written 11 Encyclicals; the last one, "Evangelium Vitae", written in 1995, defends life, speaking out against abortion, euthanasia and the death penalty. On October 11, 1992, after long consultation and labor with the world episcopacy, he signed the New Catechism of the Catholic Church, later translated into every language. He has nominated dozens of cardinals and, in view of the third millennium, has summoned numerous bishop synods. He has acted as a leader in events that have changed the world, i.e. on December 1 1989, he received Mikhail Gorbachev, President of USSR. He also refused to be crowned with a tiara; the tiara was used for the last time with Pope Paul VI.

Pope John Paul II has officially announced the celebration of the Jubilee for the year 2000 with his apostolic letter "Tertio Millenio adveniente", dated November 24, 1994. During a trip to Cuba in 1998, he met with Fidel Castro. For the first time in history, the Papal Bull dated January, 29, 1998 proclaimed that the Holy Year for the year 2000 would be celebrated contemporaneously in Rome as well as in the Holy Land, and in local churches. The Holy Doors at St. Peter's will be opened during midnight mass on December 24, 1999 and the Jubilee will end on January 6, 2001. Including his trip to Mexico City on January 22, 1999, the Pope is estimated to have travelled a total of 100 000 kilometres during 85 international tours, the equivalent of having travelled 28 times around the world.

THE POPES IN CHRONOLOGICAL ORDER

The names without numbers belong to the Popes that have never
been acknowledged and are considered to be Anti-popes.

1)	ST. PETER (42-67)
2)	ST. LINUS (67-76)
3)	ST. CLETUS (76-88)
4)	ST. CLEMENT I (88-97)
5)	ST. EVARISTUS (97-105)
6)	ST. ALEXANDER I (105-115)
7)	ST. SIXTUS I (115-125)
8)	ST. TELESPHORUS (125-136)
9)	ST. HYGINUS (136-140)
10)	ST. PIUS I (140-155)
11)	ST. ANICETUS (155-166)
12)	ST. SOTER (166-175)
13)	ST. ELEUTHERIUS (175-189)
14)	ST. VICTOR I (189-199)
15)	ST. ZEPHYRINUS (199-217)
16)	ST. CALLISTUS (217-222)
	HIPPOLYTUS St. (217-235)
17)	ST. URBAN I (222-230)
18)	ST. PONTIAN (230-235)
19)	ST. ANTERUS (235-236)
20)	ST. FABIAN (236-250)
21)	ST. CORNELIUS (251-253)
	NOVATIANUS (251)
22)	ST. LUCIUS I (253-254)
23)	ST. STEPHEN I (254-257)
24)	ST. SIXTUS II (257-258)
25)	ST. DIONYSIUS (256-268)
26)	ST. FELIX I (269-274)
27)	ST. EUTYCHIAN (275-283)
28)	ST. CAIUS (283-296)
29)	ST. MARCELLINUS (296-304)
30)	ST. MARCELLUS I (308-309)
31)	ST. EUSEBIUS (309)
32)	ST. MILTIADES (311-314)
	or MELCHIADES
33)	ST. SILVESTER I (314-335)
34)	ST. MARK (336)
35)	ST. JULIUS I (337-352)
36)	LIBERIUS (352-366)
	FELIX II (355-365)
37)	ST. DAMASUS I (366-384)
	URSINUS (366-384)
38)	ST. SIRICIUS (384-399)
39)	ST. ANASTASIUS I (399-401)
40)	ST. INNOCENT I (401-417)
41)	ST. ZOSIMUS (417-418)

42)	ST. BONIFACE I (418-422)
	EULALIO (418-419)
43)	ST. CELESTINE I (422-432)
44)	ST. SIXTUS III (432-440)
45)	ST.LEO I (440-461)
46)	ST. HILARUS (461-468)
47)	ST. SIMPLICIUS (468-483)
48)	ST. FELIX III (483-492)
49)	ST. GELASIUS I (492-496)
50)	ANASTASIUS II (496-498)
51)	ST. SYMMACHUS (498-514)
	LAURENCE (498-501-505)
52)	ST. HORMISDAS (514-523)
53)	ST. JOHN I (523-526)
54)	ST. FELIX IV (526-530)
55)	BONIFACE II (530-532)
	DIOSCORO (530)
56)	JOHN II (533-535)
57)	AGAPITUS I (535-536)
58)	ST. SILVERIUS (536-537)
59)	VIGILIUS (537-555)
60)	PELAGIUS I (556-561)
61)	JOHN III (561-574)
62)	BENEDICT I (575-579)
63)	PELAGIUS II (579-590)
64)	ST. GREGORY I (590-604)
65)	SABINIAN (604-606)
66)	BONIFACE III (607)
67)	ST. BONIFACE IV (608-615)
68)	ST. ADEODATUS (615-618)
	or DEUSDEIT I
69)	BONIFACE V (619-625)
70)	HONORIUS I (625-638)
71)	SEVERINUS (640)
72)	JOHN IV (640-642)
73)	THEODORE I (642-649)
74)	ST. MARTIN I (649-655)
75)	ST. EUGENE I (654-657)
76)	ST. VITALIAN (657-672)
77)	ADEODATUS II (672-676)
78)	DONUS (676-678)
79)	ST. AGATHO (678-681)
80)	ST. LEO II (682-683)
81)	ST. BENEDICT II (684-685)
82)	JOHN V (685-686)
83)	CONON (686-687)

	THEODORE (687)
	PASCHAL (687)
84)	ST. SERGIUS I (687-701)
85)	JOHN VI (701-705)
86)	JOHN VII (705-707)
87)	SISSINIUS (708)
88)	CONSTANTINE (708-715)
89)	ST. GREGORY II (715-731)
90)	ST. GREGORY III (731-741)
91)	ST. ZACHARIAS (741-752)
92)	STEPHEN II (752-757)
93)	ST. PAUL I (757-767)
	CONSTANTINE (767-769)
	PHILIP (768)
94)	STEPHEN III (768-772)
95)	HADRIAN I (772-795)
96)	ST. LEO III (795-816)
97)	STEPHEN IV (816-817)
98)	ST. PASCHAL I (817-824)
99)	EUGENE II (824-827)
100)	VALENTINE (827)
101)	GREGORY IV (827-844)
	JOHN (844)
102)	SERGIUS II (844-847)
103)	ST. LEO IV (847-855)
104)	BENEDICT III (855-858)
	ANASTASIUS (855-880)
105)	ST. NICHOLAS (858-867)
106)	HADRIAN II (867-872)
107)	JOHN VIII (872-882)
108)	MARINUS I (882-884)
109)	ST.HADRIAN III (884-885)
110)	STEPHEN V (885-891)
111)	FORMOSUS (891-896)
112)	BONIFACE VI (896)
113)	STEPHEN VI (896-897)
114)	ROMANUS (897)
115)	THEODORE II (897)
116)	JOHN IX (898-900)
117)	BENEDICT IV (900-903)
118)	LEO V (903)
	CHRISTOPHER (903-904)
119)	SERGIUS III (904-911)
120)	ANASTASIUS III (911-913)
121)	LANDO (913-914)
122)	JONH X (914-928)

123) LEO VI (928)
124) STEPHEN VII (928-931)
125) JOHN XI (931-935)
126) LEO VII (936-939)
127) STEPHEN VIII (939-942)
128) MARINUS II (942-946)
129) AGAPITUS II (946-955)
130) JONH XII (955-964)
131) LEO VIII (963-965)
132) BENEDICT V (964-966)
133) JOHN XIII (965-972)
134) BENEDICT VI (973-974)
   BONIFACE VII (974-985)
135) BENEDICT VII (974-983)
136) JOHN XIV (983-984)
137) JOHN XV (985-996)
138) GREGORY V (996-999)
   JOHN XVI (997-998)
139) SILVESTER II (999-1003)
140) JOHN XVII (1003)
141) JOHN XVIII (1004-1009)
142) SERGIUS IV (1009-1012)
143) BENEDICT VIII (1012-1024)
   GREGORY (1012)
144) JOHN XIX (1024-1032)
145) BENEDICT IX (1032-1044)
146) SILVESTER III (1045)
147) BENEDICT IX (1045)
148) GREGORY VI (1045-1046)
149) CLEMENT II (1046-1047)
150) BENEDICT IX (1047-1048)
151) DAMASUS II (1048)
152) ST. LEO IX (1049-1054)
153) VICTOR II (1055-1057)
154) STEPHEN IX (1057-1058)
   BENEDICT X (1058-1059)
155) NICHOLAS II (1059-1061)
156) ALEXANDER II (1061-1073)
   HONORIUS II (1061-1072)
157) ST. GREGORY VII (1073-1085)
   CLEMENT III (1084-1100)
158) BL. VICTOR III (1086-1087)
159) BL. URBAN II (1088-1099)
160) PASCHAL II (1099-1118)
   THEODORIC (1100-1102)
   ALBERT (1102)
   SYLVESTER IV (1105-1111)
161) GELASIUS II (1118-1119)
   GREGORY VII (1118-1121)
162) CALLISTUS II (1119-1124)
163) HONORIUS II (1124-1130)
   CELESTINE II (1124)
164) INNOCENT II (1130-1143)
   CLETUS II (1130-1138)
   VICTOR IV (1138)
165) CELESTINE II (1143-1144)

166) LUCIUS II (1144-1145)
167) BL. EUGENE III (1145-1153)
168) ANASTASIUS IV (1153-1154)
169) HADRIAN IV (1154-1159)
170) ALEXANDER III (1159-1181)
   VICTOR IV (1159-1164)
   PASCHAL III (1164-1168)
   CALLISTUS III (1168-1178)
   INNOCENT III (1179-1180)
171) LUCIUS III (1181-1185)
172) URBAN III (1185-1187)
173) GREGORY VIII (1187)
174) CLEMENT III (1187-1191)
175) CELESTINE III (1191-1198)
176) INNOCENT III (1198-1216)
177) HONORIUS III (1216-1227)
178) GREGORY IX (1227-1241)
179) CELESTINE IV (1241)
180) INNOCENT IV (1243-1254)
181) ALEXANDER IV (1254-1261)
182) URBAN IV (1261-1264)
183) CLEMENT IV (1265-1268)
184) BL. GREGORY X (1272-1276)
185) BL. INNOCENT V (1276)
186) HADRIAN V (1276)
187) JOHN XXI (1276-1277)
188) NICHOLAS III (1277-1280)
189) MARTIN IV (1281-1285)
190) HONORIUS IV (1285-1287)
191) NICHOLAS IV (1288-1292)
192) ST. CELESTINE V (1294)
193) BONIFACE VIII (1294-1303)
194) BL. BENEDICT XI (1303-1304)
195) CLEMENT V (1305-1314)
196) JOHN XXII (1316-1334)
   NICHOLAS V (1328-1333)
197) BENEDICT XII (1335-1342)
198) CLEMENT VI (1342-1352)
199) INNOCENT VI (1352-1362)
200) BL. URBAN V (1362-1370)
201) GREGORY XI (1371-1378)
202) URBAN VI (1378-1389)
203) BONIFACE IX (1389-1404)
204) INNOCENT VII (1404-1406)
205) GREGORY XII (1406-1415)
   CLEMENT VII (1378-1394)
   BENEDICT XIII (1394-1423)
   ALEXANDER V (1409-1410)
   JOHN XXIII (1410-1415)
206) MARTIN V (1417-1431)
207) EUGENE IV (1431-1447)
   FELIX V (1440.1449)
208) NICHOLAS V (1447-1455)
209) CALIXTUS III (1455-1458)
210) PIUS II (1458-1464)
211) PAUL II (1464-1471)

212) SIXTUS IV (1471-1484)
213) INNOCENT VIII (1484-1492)
214) ALEXANDER VI (1492-1503)
215) PIUS III (1503)
216) JULIUS II (1503-1513)
217) LEO X (1513-1521)
218) HADRIAN VI (1522-1523)
219) CLEMENT VII (1523-1534)
220) PAUL III (1534-1549)
221) JULES III (1550-1555)
222) MARCELLUS II (1555)
223) PAUL IV (1555-1559)
224) PIUS IV (1560-1565)
225) ST. PIUS V (1566-1572)
226) GREGORY XIII (1572-1585)
227) SIXTUS V (1585-1590)
228) URBAN VII (1590)
229) GREGORY XIV (1590-1591)
230) INNOCENT IX (1591)
231) CLEMENT VIII (1592-1605)
232) LEO XI (1605)
233) PAUL V (1605-1621)
234) GREGORY XV (1621-1623)
235) URBAN VIII (1623-1644)
236) INNOCENT X (1644-1655)
237) ALEXANDER VII (1655-1667)
238) CLEMENT IX (1667-1669)
239) CLEMENT X (1669-1676)
240) BL. INNOCENT XI (1676-1689)
241) ALEXANDER VIII (1689-1691)
242) INNOCENT XII (1691-1700)
243) CLEMENT XI (1700-1721)
244) INNOCENT XIII (1721-1724)
245) BENEDICT XIII (1724-1730)
246) CLEMENT XII (1730-1740)
247) BENEDICT XIV (1740-1758)
248) CLEMENT XIII (1758-1769)
249) CLEMENT XIV (1769-1774)
250) PIUS VI (1775-1799)
251) PIUS VII (1800-1823)
252) LEO XII (1823-1829)
253) PIUS VIII (1829-1830)
254) GREGORY XVI (1831-1846)
255) PIUS IX (1846-1878)
256) LEO XIII (1878-1903)
257) ST. PIUS X (1903-1914)
258) BENEDICT XV (1914-1922)
259) PIUS XI (1922-1939)
260) PIUS XII (1939-1958)
261) JOHN XXIII (1959-1963)
262) PAUL VI (1963-1978)
263) JOHN PAUL I (1978)
264) JOHN PAUL II (1978-

(From the 1966 Pontifical annual)

THE POPES IN ALPHABETICAL ORDER

The names without numbers belong to the Popes that have never been acknowledged and are considered to be Anti-popes.

A

68) ADEODATUS I (615-618)
or DEUSDEIT I
77) ADEODATUS II (672-676)
57) AGAPITUS I (535-536)
129) AGAPITUS II (946-955)
79) AGATHO (678-681)
ALBERT (1102)
6) ALEXANDER I (105-115)
156) ALEXANDER II (1061-1073)
170) ALEXANDER III (1159-1181)
181) ALEXANDER IV (1254-1261)
ALEXANDER V (1409-1410)
214) ALEXANDER VI (1492-1503)
237) ALEXANDER VII (1655-1667)
241) ALEXANDER VIII (1689-1691)
3) ANACLETUS (76-88)
ANASTASIUS (855-880)
39) ANASTASIUS I (399-401)
50) ANASTASIUS II (496-498)
120) ANASTASIUS III (911-913)
168) ANASTASIUS IV (1153-1154)
11) ANICETUS (155-166)
19) ANTERUS (235-236)

B

62) BENEDICT I (575-579)
81) BENEDICT II (684-685)
104) BENEDICT III (855-858)
117) BENEDICT IV (900-903)
132) BENEDICT V (964-966)
134) BENEDICT VI (973-974)
135) BENEDICT VII (974-983)
143) BENEDICT VIII (1012-1024)
145) BENEDICT IX (1032-1044)
147) BENEDICT IX (1045)
150) BENEDICT IX (1047-1048)
BENEDICT X (1058-1059)
194) BENEDICT XI (1303-1304)
197) BENEDICT XII (1335-1342)
BENEDICT XIII (1394-1423)
245) BENEDICT XIII (1724-1730)
247) BENEDICT XIV (1740-1758)
258) BENEDICT XV (1914-1922)

B (continued)

42) BONIFACE I (418-422)
55) BONIFACE II (530-532)
66) BONIFACE III (607)
67) BONIFACE IV (608-615)
69) BONIFACE V (619-625)
112) BONIFACE VI (896)
BONIFACE VII (974-985)
193) BONIFACE VIII (1294-1303)
203) BONIFACE IX (1389-1404)

C

28) CAIUS (283-296)
16) CALLISTUS I (217-222)
162) CALLISTUS II (1119-1124)
209) CALLISTUS III (1455-1458)
CALLISTUS III (1168-1178)
43) CELESTINE I (422-432)
165) CELESTINE II (1143-1144)
CELESTINE II (1124)
175) CELESTINE III (1191-1198)
179) CELESTINE IV (1241)
192) CELESTINE V (1294)
CHRISTOPHER (903-904)
4) CLEMENT I (88-97)
149) CLEMENT II (1046-1047)
174) CLEMENT III (1187-1191)
CLEMENT III (1084-1100)
183) CLEMENT IV (1265-1268)
195) CLEMENT V (1305-1314)
198) CLEMENT VI (1342-1352)
219) CLEMENT VII (1523-1534)
CLEMENT VII (1378-1394)
231) CLEMENT VIII (1592-1605)
238) CLEMENT IX (1667-1669)
239) CLEMENT X (1669-1676)
243) CLEMENT XI (1700-1721)
246) CLEMENT XII (1730-1740)
248) CLEMENT XIII (1758-1769)
249) CLEMENT XIV (1769-1774)
CLETUS II (1130-1138)
83) CONON (686-687)
88) CONSTANTINE (708-715)
CONSTANTINE (767- 769)
21) CORNELIUS (251-253)

D

37) DAMASUS I (366-384)
151) DAMASUS II (1048)
25) DIONYSIUS (256-268)
DIOSCORO (530)
78) DONUS (676-678)

E

13) ELEUTHERIUS (175-189)
75) EUGENE I (654-657)
99) EUGENE II (824-827)
167) EUGENE III (1145-1153)
207) EUGENE IV (1431-1447)
31) EUSEBIUS (309)
EULALIO (418- 419)
27) EUTYCHIAN (275-283)
5) EVARISTUS (97-105)

F

20) FABIAN (236-250)
26) FELIX I (269-274)
FELIX II (355-365)
48) FELIX III (483-492)
54) FELIX IV (526-530)
FELIX V (1440-1449)
111) FORMOSUS (891-896)

G

49) GELASIUS I (492-496)
161) GELASIUS II (1118-1119)
GREGORY (1012)
64) GREGORY I (590-604)
89) GREGORY II (715-731)
90) GREGORY III (731-741)
101) GREGORY IV (827-844)
138) GREGORY V (966-999)
148) GREGORY VI (1045-1046)
157) GREGORY VII (1073-1085)
173) GREGORY VIII (1187)
GREGORY VIII (1118-1121)
178) GREGORY IX (1227-1241)
184) GREGORY X (1272-1276)
201) GREGORY XI (1371-1378)

205) GREGORY XII (1406-1415)	137) JOHN XV (985-996)	*NICHOLAS V (1328-1330)*
226) GREGORY XIII (1572-1585)	*JOHN XVI (997-998)*	*NOVATIANUS (251)*
229) GREGORY XIV (1590-1591)	140) JOHN XVII (1003)	
234) GREGORY XV (1621-1623)	141) JOHN XVIII (1004-1009)	

H

95) HADRIAN I (772-795)
106) HADRIAN II (867-872)
109) HADRIAN III (884-885)
169) HADRIAN IV (1154-1159)
186) HADRIAN V (1276)
218) HADRIAN VI (1522-1523)
46) HILARUS (461-468)
ST. HIPPOLYTUS (217-235)
70) HONORIUS I (625-638)
163) HONORIUS II (1124-1130)
HONORIUS II (1061-1072)
177) HONORIUS III (1216-1227)
190) HONORIUS IV (1285-1287)
52) HORMISDAS (514-523)
9) HYGINUS (136-140)

I

40) INNOCENT I (401-417)
164) INNOCENT II (1130-1143)
176) INNOCENT III (1198-1216)
INNOCENT III (1179-1180)
180) INNOCENT IV (1243-1254)
185) INNOCENT V (1276)
199) INNOCENT VI (1352-1362)
204) INNOCENT VII (1404-1406)
213) INNOCENT VIII (1484-1492)
230) INNOCENT IX (1591)
236) INNOCENT X (1644-1655)
240) INNOCENT XI (1676-1689)
242) INNOCENT XII (1691-1700)
244) INNOCENT XIII (1721-1724)

J

JOHN (844)
53) JOHN I (523-526)
56) JOHN II (533-535)
61) JOHN III (561-574)
72) JOHN IV (640-642)
82) JOHN V (685-686)
85) JOHN VI (701-705)
86) JOHN VII (705-707)
107) JOHN VIII (872-882)
116) JOHN IX (898-900)
122) JONH X (914-928)
125) JOHN XI (931-935)
130) JONH XII (955-964)
133) JOHN XIII (965-972)
136) JOHN XIV (983-984)

144) JOHN XIX (1024-1032)
187) JOHN XXI (1276-1277)
196) JOHN XXII (1316-1334)
261) JOHN XXIII (1958-1963)
JOHN XXIII (1410-1415)
263) JOHN PAUL I (1978)
264) JOHN PAUL II (1978-
35) JULIUS I (337-352)
216) JULIUS II (1503-1513)
221) JULIUS III (1550-1555)

L

121) LANDO (913-914)
LAURENCE (498-501-505)
45) LEO I (440-461)
80) LEO II (682-683)
96) LEO III (795-816)
103) LEO IV (847-855)
118) LEO V (903)
123) LEO VI (928)
126) LEO VII (936-939)
131) LEO VIII (963-965)
152) LEO IX (1049-1054)
217) LEO X (1513-1521)
232) LEO XI (1605)
252) LEO XII (1823-1829)
256) LEO XIII (1878-1903)
36) LIBERIUS (352-366)
2) LINUS (67-76)
22) LUCIUS I (253-254)
166) LUCIUS II (1144-1145)
171) LUCIUS III (1181-1185)

M

29) MARCELLINUS (296-304)
30) MARCELLUS I (308-309)
222) MARCELLUS II (1555)
108) MARINUS I (882-884)
128) MARINUS II (942-946)
34) MARK (336)
74) MARTIN I (649-655)
189) MARTIN IV (1281-1285)
206) MARTIN V (1417-1431)
32) MILTIADES (311-314)

N

105) NICHOLAS I (858-867)
155) NICHOLAS II (1059-1061)
188) NICHOLAS III (1277-1280)
191) NICHOLAS IV (1288-1292)
208) NICHOLAS V (1447-1455)

P

PASCHAL (687)
98) PASCHAL I (817-824)
160) PASCHAL II (1099-1118)
PASCHAL III (1164-1168)
93) PAUL I (757-767)
211) PAUL II (1464-1471)
220) PAUL III (1534-1549)
223) PAUL IV (1555-1559)
233) PAUL V (1605-1621)
262) PAUL VI (1963-1978)
60) PELAGIUS I (556-561)
63) PELAGIUS II (579-590)
1) PETER (42-67)
PHILIP (768)
10) PIUS I (140-155)
210) PIUS II (1458-1464)
215) PIUS III (1503)
224) PIUS IV (1560-1565)
225) PIUS V (1566-1572)
250) PIUS VI (1775-1799)
251) PIUS VII (1800-1823)
253) PIUS VIII (1829-1830)
255) PIUS IX (1846-1878)
257) PIUS X (1903-1914)
259) PIUS XI (1922-1939)
260) PIUS XII (1939-1958)
18) PONTIAN (230-235)

R

114) ROMANUS (897)

S

65) SABINIAN (604-606)
84) SERGIUS I (687-701)
102) SERGIUS II (844-847)
119) SERGIUS III (904-911)
142) SERGIUS IV (1009-1012)
71) SEVERINUS (640)
58) SILVERIUS (536-537)
33) SILVESTER I (314-335)
139) SILVESTER II (999-1003)
146) SILVESTER III (1045)
SILVESTER IV (1105-1111)
47) SIMPLICIUS (468-483)
38) SIRICIUS (384-399)
87) SISSINIUS (708)
7) SIXTUS I (115-125)
24) SIXTUS II (257-258)
44) SIXTUS III (432-440)
212) SIXTUS IV (1471-1484)
227) SIXTUS V (1585-1590)

12) SOTER (166-175)	73) THEODORE I (642-649)
23) STEPHEN I (254-257)	115) THEODORE II (897)
92) STEPHEN II (752-757)	*THEODORIC (1100-1102)*
94) STEPHEN III (768-772)	
97) STEPHEN IV (816-817)	
110) STEPHEN V (885-891)	

V

100) VALENTINE (827)	
14) VICTOR I (189-199)	
153) VICTOR II (1055-1057)	
158) VICTOR III (1086-1087)	

12) SOTER (166-175)
23) STEPHEN I (254-257)
92) STEPHEN II (752-757)
94) STEPHEN III (768-772)
97) STEPHEN IV (816-817)
110) STEPHEN V (885-891)
113) STEPHEN VI (896-897)
124) STEPHEN VII (928-931)
127) STEPHEN VIII (939-942)
154) STEPHEN IX (1057-1058)
51) SYMMACHUS (498-514)

T

8) TELESPHORUS (125-136)
THEODORE (687)

73) THEODORE I (642-649)
115) THEODORE II (897)
THEODORIC (1100-1102)

U

17) URBAN I (222-230)
159) URBAN II (1088-1099)
172) URBAN III (1185-1187)
182) URBAN IV (1261-1264)
200) URBAN V (1362-1370)
202) URBAN VI (1378-1389)
228) URBAN VII (1590)
235) URBAN VIII (1623-1644)
URSINUS (366-384)

V

100) VALENTINE (827)
14) VICTOR I (189-199)
153) VICTOR II (1055-1057)
158) VICTOR III (1086-1087)
VICTOR IV (1138)
VICTOR IV (1159-1164)
59) VIGILIUS (537-555)
76) VITALIAN (657-672)

Z

91) ZACHARIAS (741-752)
15) ZEPHYRINUS (199-217)
41) ZOSIMUS (417-418)

THE ANTI-POPES

The Popes not officially acknowledged (opposed to the official Popes).
The number before the name refers to the official Pope against whose government the Anti-pope was elected.

(16) *ST. HIPPOLYTUS (217-235)*
(21) *NOVATIANUS (251)*
(36) *FELIX II (355-365)*
(37) *URSINUS (366-384)*
(42) *EULALIO (418- 419)*
(51) *LAURENCE (498-501-505)*
(55) *DIOSCORO (530)*
(83) *THEODORE (687)*
(84) *PASCHAL (687)*
(93) *CONSTANTINE (767- 769)*
(95) *PHILIP (768)*
(101) *JOHN (844)*
(104) *ANASTASIUS (855-880)*

(118) *CHRISTOPHER (903-904)*
(134) *BONIFACE VII (974-985)*
(138) *JOHN XVI (997-998)*
(143) *GREGORY (1012)*
(154) *BENEDICT X (1058-1059)*
(156) *HONORIUS II (1061-1072)*
(157) *CLEMENT III (1084-1100)*
(160) *THEODORIC (1100-1102)*
(160) *ALBERT (1102)*
(160) *SILVESTER IV (1105-1111)*
(161) *GREGORY VIII (1118-1121)*
(163) *CELESTINE II (1124)*
(164) *CLETUS II (1130-1138)*

(165) *VICTOR IV (1138)*
(170) *VICTOR IV (1159-1164)*
(170) *PASCHAL III,1164-1168)*
(171) *CALLISTUS III (1168-1178)*
(171) *INNOCENT III (1179-1180)*
(196) *NICHOLAS V (1328-1330)*
(205) *CLEMENT VII (1378-1394)*
(205) *BENEDICT XIII (1394-1423)*
(206) *ALEXANDER V (1409-1410)*
(206) *JOHN XXIII (1410-1415)*
(207) *FELIX V (1440-1449)*

The central nave of the St. Peter's Basilica during voting at the Ecumenical Vatican II Council. More than 3000 people between council members and guests.

THE GREAT
ECUMENICAL
COUNCILS

"DE CONCILIO OECUMENICO"

Council, from the Latin concilium "convocation, assembly", comp. cum "together" with clamare "to convoke, to call".

Councils are legally convened assemblies of ecclesiastical dignitaries and theological experts for the purpose of discussing and regulating matters of church doctrine and discipline.

There are four kind of Councils: Diocesan Synod, convoked by the bishop; Provincial Council, convoked by the Metropolite; National Council, convoked by the Patriach or Church Primate of the relevant nation; Ecumenical Council, convoked by the Pope.

The Ecumenical Council is divided into three stages as established by the code of Canon Law.

The Council has to be convoked by the Pope in order to be legitimate.

1st stage: The convocation

The following are convoked with the right to vote: Cardinals of the S.R.C., Patriarchs, Primates, Archbishops and Bishops, Abbots and Primate Abbots, Superior Abbots and generals of Religious Orders.

2nd stage: The celebration

It Happens under the presidency of the Pope or his legates. Only the Pope has the authority to establish the conciliar activities and the examination order of the topics to be discussed. He has the faculty to wind-up the council and to adjourn or to transfer it to another seat.

3rd stage: The confirmation

The council has to be approved by the Pope in order to become legitimate. Once the decisions of the council have received the papal confirmation they bind all Christians.

The Council results and regulations are invested by the authority of the Pope and the whole assembly.

The early Christian community used to convene to decide the election of the presbyters, listen to the prophets and settle points of political and religious nature.

As the Church and the ecclesiastic hierarchy grew, every deliberation progressively ended up in the hands of the clergy. From the beginning of the third century, the councils were no longer attended by the church followers but only by the bishops. The first ecumenical council in Nicaea (325 A.D.) was convoked by Constantine with the intent of deciding on Trinitarian doctrine.

The ecumenical councils play a dominant role in the history of the Church. In the 13th century, under the pressure of the political rebellion against the Church, a counciliar doctrine was established which conferred upon the council the supreme power to depose the Pope. The Catholic Church acknowledges some of the Councils and refuses to accept those that were not convoked by a Pope (it is worth noting that until the 10th century only the Emperors had the power to convoke a Council). Starting from the 2nd council of Ephesus, the Western and Eastern Churches have acknowledged seven councils; the Eastern Church adds an 8th (Constantinople IV, 869) which establishes the independence of the Eastern Church. The Counciliar tradition continues in the Western Church all the way to the XXI Council (Vatican II).

1°
FIRST COUNCIL OF NICAEA
325 A.D.
May 20 - August 25

POPE
SILVESTER I (33)

EMPEROR
CONSTANTINE THE GREAT

Convoked by Emperor Constantine to defend the Christian Faith. Three hundred and eighteen bishops were present, amongst these were Vincent and Vitus who assisted as legates of Pope Silvester. The Aryan doctrine was condemned and the

Divinity of the Word Incarnate, the equal nature of Jesus and God the Father, was defined. The date for keeping Easter (against the Quartodecimas) was fixed.

Contemporary events:
- Consecration of the first Haghia Sophia in Constantinople, the new capital (325).
- Prince Crispus, son of Constantine I, is sentenced to death.
- Emperor Constantine I builds the Basilica of San Giovanni in Laterano on top of the old Laterani family palaces.

A recomposition of the Council of Nicae from a 16th century frescoe in the Church of St. Martino ai Monti.

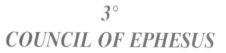

2°
FIRST COUNCIL
OF CONSTANTINOPLE

381 A.D.
May - July

POPE	EMPEROR
ST. DAMASUS I (37)	*THEODOSIUS I*

In 381, the Emperor Theodosius convoked the first Council of Constantinople to put an end to the confusion created by the Aryan heresy and by the followers of the Maratonians, Acacians and Sabellians. Due to the existing political climate, only 150 bishops attended the council. Pope Damasus and the western bishops were not present. The divinity of the Holy Spirit was defined. The dogmatic concepts of the three entities of the Trinity as well as the unity of the divine essence, in the Father, the Son and the Holy Spirit were settled. Rome was awarded the supremacy over all the other churches.

Contemporary events:
- St. Jerolamus translates "The Bible" adopted by the Church.
- Wulfila, bishop of the Goths, dies (383); he had written treatises, invented the gothic script and translated part of the Holy Scriptures.

The great Roman Emperor of the Orient Theodosius 1. Coin.

3°
COUNCIL OF EPHESUS

431 A.D.
June 22 - July 21

POPE	EMPEROR
ST. CELESTINE I (43)	*THEODOSIUS II*

The city of Ephesus, in Anatolia, where the apostles Peter and Paul spent part of their apostolic life, hosted the third council under the protection of Emperor Theodosius II. Bishop Cyril of Alexandria came to represent Pope Celestinus I: more than 50 bishops (from a total of 198) came from Northern Africa, where the Christian faith was strongly thriving. The council condemned patriarch John of Anthiochia and Nestorius of Constantinople, who proclaimed Jesus was only a man in whom the Word resided and Mary was not God's mother. The council declared Mary the mother of God, defined the true personal unity of Christ and affirmed that Jesus was the Supreme Minister.

Contemporary events:
- Attila becomes King of the Huns (434).
- St. Augustin dies (430).
- Proclus Diodorus devises a method for mapping out the earth's meridians.

The crowning of Mary, from a mosaic made by Torriti (1295), located in the apse of Santa Maria Maggiore in Rome.

4°
COUNCIL OF CHALCEDON

451 A.D.
October 8 - November 1st

POPE	**EMPEROR**
ST. LEO I (45)	*MARCIAN I AND PUCHERIAS*

This was the most important council of time of the Fathers of the Church because of the large number of bishops that participated: about 600. They condemned the Euthychian heresy that substained the divine nature of Christ to the point of obliterating his human side. The christologic dogma that defined the two natures was proclaimed and accepted. The series of dogmatic councils ended on November 1st in Chalcedon: Gregory the Great compared them to the Four Gospels.

Contemporary events:
- The battle of the Catalaunici fields in France (Champagne) 451 between Aetius and Attila. As a result ,the power of Attila is curtailed and Roman dominance over Gall is restored.

The colossal statue of the Emperor Marcian Flavius, Greek saint, at Barletta.

5°
SECOND COUNCIL OF CONSTANTINOPLE

553 A.D.
May 5 - June 2nd

POPE	**EMPEROR**
VIGILIUS (59)	*JUSTINIAN I AND THEODORA*

While the Western Roman Empire was crumbling under the barbarian invasions, Justinian was worried by the heresies which impended on his empire. It was a period of Byzantine splendour and Justinian with his strong personality was the ruler of politics; he was able to open the Council of Constantinople against the will of Pope Vigilius. The main topic of the council was about certain writings (The Three Chapters) of Theodoret, Theodor and Ibas which defended Nestorius. Notwithstanding the Consistum, the Pope, pressured by the Emperor, condemned the three nestorians.

Contemporary events:
- The Franks invade Italy. Narses defeats them and makes Italy a province of the Eastern Empire (533);

Emperor Justinian and his wife Theodora depicted with their retinue. Mosaic located in the church of St. Vitale in Ravenna.

6°
THIRD COUNCIL OF CONSTANTINOPLE

680 A.D.
November 7, 680 - September 16, 681

POPE *ST. AGATHO (79)*	**EMPEROR** *CONSTANTINE IV*

It was held in the great imperial palace in Constantinople. The 174 bishops attending were all from the Byzantine empire. Pope Agatho sent, from Rome, a profession of faith regarding duothelism; as a consequence, the Council put an end to monothelism by defining two wills in Christ, the Divine and the human, as two distinct principles of operation. Pope Honorius I was cancelled from the list of heretics. Bishop Macarius persisted in the monotheistic theory and was therefore condemned and deposed from his office.

Contemporary events:
- The Arabs give up the siege of Constantinople (678).
- Pippin reunites the kingdom of the Franks (687).

Emperor Constantine with the Conciliar Fathers. Miniature from the Vatican Codes.

7°
COUNCIL OF NICAEA
787 A.D.
September 24 - October 23

POPE	**EMPEROR**
HADRIAN I (95)	*IRINE AND CONSTANTINE V*

Under the Emperor Leo III the iconoclasts were persecuted because of their offensive worship of God. Empress Irine, mother of Constantine VI, and pope Hadrian convoked the Council to foster religious peace and unity in the Orient. 330 bishops took part in the council along with many monks. A decision was reached that established that adoration was only for God and veneration for the saints, cross and holy relics. At the closing of the Council, it was declared that "the more a faithful follower looks at the images the more he shall remember the One who is depicted in them."

Contemporary events:
- Widukind, Duke of Saxony, is baptized (785).
- Charles the Great is crowned Emperor of Rome (800).

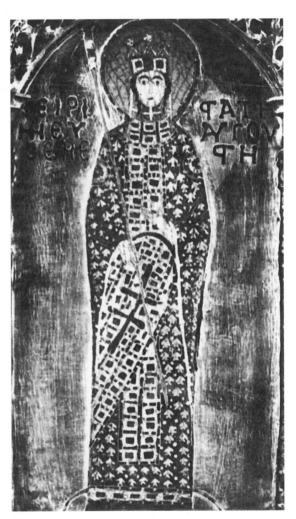

Empress Irine, wife of Leo IV and Regent for Constantine's younger son (from a golden altar-piece, S. Marco, Venice).

8°
FOURTH COUNCIL OF CONSTANTINOPLE

869 A.D.
October 5, 869 - February 28, 870

POPE
HADRIAN II (106)

EMPEROR
BASIL I

With the help of Emperor Michael III, Photius, self-proclaimed bishop of Constantinople, deposed Ignatius. The ensuing conflicts and massacres-culminated with the siege of Michael III and the rise to power of Basil the Macedonian. Ten years later the schism was solved but the expansion of Constantinople did not guarantee a solid union with Rome. Photius accused the Pope of having added the word "filioque" in the Nicene creed to affirm that the Holy Spirit proceeds from the Father to the Son (not from the Father through the Son).

He also excommunicated Pope Nicholas I during the Synod of Constantinople. The successor of Hadrian the II accepted the ruling of the Council of Constantinople. In the last session, the council decided upon the solemn definition for the Councils, calling them "Ecumenical".

Contemporary events:
- Alfred the Great elected King of Wessex, Kingdom of the Saxons (871).
- The Norwegians colonize Iceland (874).
- The Normans invade the continent.

The church of St. Sophie in Constantinople where the Council was held.

FIRST LATERAN COUNCIL

1123 A.D.
March 18 - March 27

POPE
CALLISTUS II (162)

EMPEROR
HENRY V

This first council of the middle ages was convoked but places and ideas were quite different from the last one. A large number of western bishops attended. This council did not defined dogmatic matters, but dealt with church discipline and ratified the Treaty of Worms in 1122, stipulated by Henry V and Calistus II, regarding the investitures. It was finally decided that the bishops and the abbots would be elected by the clergy and would subsequently be approved by the sovereigns. The council was held in the Basilica of St. Giovanni, which was the Pope's residence at that time. 300 bishops attended who condemned all forms of simony and concubinage for ecclesiasticals, included the Bishop Corrado of Constance in the saint's catalogue, and condemned all usurers and blood related marriages.

Contemporary events:
- The first Council convoked by a Pope (1122).
- Agreement of the Treaty of Worms (1122).
- The Emperor Henry V dies (1125).

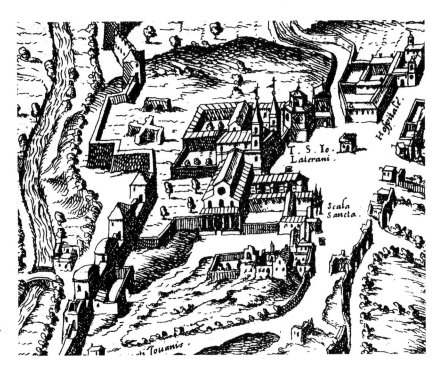

Basilica of St. Giovanni in Laterano. Drawing from a map of Rome by Du Perac.

10°
SECOND LATERAN COUNCIL
1139 A.D.
April 2 - April 17

POPE	EMPEROR
INNOCENT II (164)	*CONRAD III*

Pope Innocent returned to Rome , with the help of Lothair, after the death of the anti-pope Anacletus II and called a Council with the aim of strengthening Christian unity. More than a thousand bishops came to Rome, very few came from Arab countries. Pope Innocent attended the council and stripped all the priests appointed by the anti-pope of their investiture. The interpretations of the Sacraments by Pietro Bruys and Henry Clumy were condemned; according to them, the Sacrament of baptism was invalid because children were incapable of an act of faith, the Sacrament of the Eucharistic was not to be performed because it was performed by Christ once and for all and wanted the Sacrament of marriage extended to priests and monks.

Contemporary events:
- Conrad III elected King of the Germans (1138).
- Battle of Weinsberg (1140).
- The Arabs conquer Edessa (1144).

Interior view of San Giovanni in Laterano the way it was at the time of the Council (from a fresco in S. Martino ai Monti, Rome).

11°
THIRD LATERAN COUNCIL

1179 A.D.
March 5 - March 19

POPE
ALEXANDER III (170)

EMPEROR
FREDERICK I (REDBEARD)

The continuous fighting between the Church and Frederick came to a peaceful agreement with the defeat of the latter in the battle of Legnano. In this council there were numerous interventions by the bishops from the Middle East and newly appointed regions such as Scotland. With a new ruling, the election of a new pope was reserved to the Sacred College. It was established that a two-thirds majority was sufficient for the nomination. The candidate elected was to be excommunicated in case of his non-acceptance of the charge. A bishop could be elected only if he was more than thirty years old and a legitimate child.

Contemporary events:
- Battle of Legnano (1176).
- Peace of Venice (1177).
- Henry the Lion is banned (1180)
- Louis VII of France dies (1180)

Frederick Redbeard, defeated in the Legnano battle, throws himself at Pope Alexander's feet
(from a painting by Spinello Aretino, Palazzo Comunale in Siena).

12°
FOURTH LATERAN COUNCIL

1215 A.D.
November 11, 1215 - July 16, 1216

POPE	EMPEROR
INNOCENT III (176)	*FREDERICK II*

Pope Innocent III witnessed the participation of 470 bishops, 800 abbots, kings and princes during this council; the Greek patriarchate of Constantinople did not attend. It condemned the Trinitarian errors of Abbot Joachim, the two natures of Christ as well as the Sacraments of Baptism, Confirmation and Holy Communion were defined. The word "Transubstantiation" was introduced in the Eucharist: the transformation of bread and wine into the body and blood of Christ. The wedding procedure and the obligation of the wedding publication were established.

Contemporary events:
- Eger's gold seal (1213).
- Otto IV is defeated at Bouvines (1214).
- Frederick II crowned at Aquisgrana (1215).
- Domenic Gudsman established the order of the Dominicans in Toulouse (1216).

The two bell towers of St. Giovanni in Laterano (13th century); the papal blessing was given from the upper loggia until the Pope's residency was transferred to the Vatican.

13°
FIRST COUNCIL OF LYONS

1245 A.D.
June 2 - July 17

POPE
INNOCENT IV (180)

EMPEROR
FREDERICK II

Because of the threats of Frederick II, Pope Innocent VI urgently called the Council of Lyons . The aim of this council was to restore order between France and the Sacred Roman Empire and the authority of the Pope. Frederick obstructed the work of the council, closed all access by land and sea to Lyons and, subsequently, the conciliars attendance was very low.

Frederick II was defined a persecutor of the Church and declared heretic.

It was decreed that Cardinals had to wear the red skull-cap as a sign of dedication and loyalty to the Church of Rome.

Contemporary events:
- The Arabs conquer Jerusalem (1244)
- Henry Raspe, count of Turingia, is anti-king in Germany (1246)
- Construction of the Cologne Cathedral begins (1248)
- The use of the clerical hat is introduced (1243)

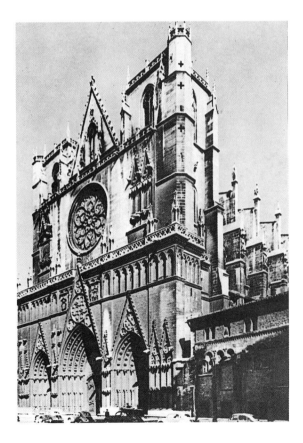

St. John the Baptist, Lyons Cathedral, where the Council was held.

14°
SECOND COUNCIL OF LYONS
1274 A.D.
May 7 - July 17

POPE	**EMPEROR**
GREGORY X (184)	*RUDOLPH V OF ABSBURG*

Pope Gregory X knew very well the reasons for the Greek schism and this was the main topic of the council: making peace with the Greek church.

More than 2000 participated: bishops, abbots, theologians, patriarchs, Eastern bishops and ambassadors from Sicily, England and Germany. The Mongolian Grand Khan sent two legates. The rules for the conclave and the papal election were laid down. The council ended with a "Te Deum" as a recognition of the reunion with the Greek church, but the reunion turned out to be very brief.

Contemporary events:
- Crusade of Louis the Saint of France (1270)
- Sicily under the hegemony of the King of Aragon (1274)
- Thomas of Aquinas dies (1274)

The Holy Spirit's symbol, in the apse of St. Peter's Basilica. Bohemian glass was used for the making of this window.

15°
COUNCIL OF VIENNE (France)
1311 A.D.
October 1st 1311 - May 1312

POPE	**EMPEROR**
CLEMENT V (195)	*HENRY VII*

Pope Clement V, pressured by King Philip, moved the Papal Seat to Avignon and convoked a Council in Vienne (France). It decided the disbandment of the Templars, an order of monks which militarily defended the Sacred Sites. The order had accumulated enormous wealth which was divided soon after. The council deliberated on a number of dogmatic and disciplinary matters: the independence of the Church, the reformation of the clergy, controls and rules about excommunication, new teaching in Universities and the celebration of the "Corpus Domini Day".

Contemporary events:
- Henry VII is crowned King in Rome (1312)
- Battle of Morgarten over the independence of Switzerland, between the Swiss and Austrian armies (1315)
- Schwyz, Uri and Unterwalden join in alliance and create the Swiss State (1315).

The Council of Vienne. Painting showing in the Sistine Hall of the Vatican.

16°
COUNCIL OF CONSTANCE
1413 A.D.
December 9, 1413 - April 22, 1418

POPE
GREGORY XII (205),
MARTIN V (206)

EMPEROR
SIGISMUND I

This council was held in one of the most obscure moments in the history of the Church: the schism of Avignon. During the past 70 years seven popes had chosen Avignon as the place for the Holy See. At one point three popes were elected contemporaneously (two of them "anti-popes", Benedict XIII and John XXIII), ensuing confusion among Catholics. Gregory XIII convoked the Council with the intent of solving this situation, under the patronage of Sigismund, King of Hungary. They put an end to the schism with the election of Martin V. The rightful

Pope confirmed the former decrees of the synod against John Hus. The authority of the Council over the Pope was defined.

Contemporary events:
- Henry V, King of England (1413).
- Battle at Azincourt (1415) during the 100 Years War between England and France.
- The defenestration of Prague (1419).
- War of the Hussits (1419-1436).

John Hus stripped of his ecclesiastical vestments is put to the stake dressed as an heretic. Manuscript of Hulrich Richental, 1460.

17°
COUNCIL OF BASLE, FERRARA, FLORENCE

1431 A.D.
July 23, 1431 - July 6, 1439

POPE
MARTIN V (206)
EUGENE IV (207)

EMPEROR
SIGISMUND I
FREDEDRICK III

The Council was initiated in Basel, transferred to Ferrara (April 9, 1438) and then to Florence only to be concluded in Rome. This council dealt with the re-union with the Greek Church, the Armenians and the Jacobites, the controversy on the conciliar theories and the compromise with the Hussits. The problems inherent to the schism of the western Church re-emerged with the death of Martin V. Eugene IV, his successor, made it clear that he was not going to accept any attacks on the Catholic Church. During his pontificate he kept the situation under control by convoking the ecumenical council again. The Pope was acknowledged as the Supreme Chief of the Universal Church, Vicary of Christ and Teacher of all Christians. The council initiated the crusade against the Turks who had invaded Hungary and occupied Constantinople.

Contemporary events:
- Burning at the stake of Joan of Arc (1431)
- Battle against the Turks at Varna (1444)
- The Turks conquer Constantinople (1453)

Reading of the Bull of union of the Greek Church with Rome; on the left Emperor Paleologo and on the right Eugene IV. Bas-relief of St. Peter's bronze door, by Filarete.

18°
FIFTH LATERAN COUNCIL
1512 A.D.
May 10 ,1512 - March 16, 1517

POPE
JULIUS II (216)
LEO X (217)

EMPEROR
LOUIS XII
MAXIMILIAN I

One hundred years had passed since the previous council and France, Germany, England and Spain were at war trying to establish their hegemony over one another. Italy was devastated by invasions of foreign armies. Julius II, a Pope of vast cultural background, was a patron of the arts and embellished Rome with the creations by Michelangelo and Raffaello and fostered the construction of the St. Peter's Basilica. He formed an alliance with Ferdinand of Spain, Henry VIII of England and the Republic of Venice to free the Holy See from the overpowering domain of France. The council condemned the attempted schism by France and established peace among the European powers.

Contemporary events:
- Christopher Columbus dies (1506)
- Michelangelo finishes the ceiling of the Sistine Chapel (1512)
- Francis I crowned King of France (1515)

The center nave of St. Giovanni in Laterano as it appeared in 1730, with the statues of the 12 apostles.

19°
COUNCIL OF TRENT

1545 A.D.
December 1st 1545 - February 28, 1563

POPE
PAUL III (220)
PIUS IV (224)

EMPEROR
CHARLES V
FERDINAND I

Convoked by Paul III, continued under Julius III (221), Marcellus II (222), Paul IV (223) closed by Pius IV (224).

This was the council that over all confirmed the continuity, universality and immortality of the Catholic Church. At the time, the catholic world was afflicted with two problems: Martin Luther and the schisms of England. The Council of Trent took actions against the Lutheran intrusion and the Protestantism condemning the errors of the reformers. This councilar action was called Counter-Reformation. This council lasted 18 years because of continuing wars and plagues. Decisions were taken against Luther and Calvin. Reformatory decrees were issued on the doctrine governing the Holy Scripture, the Original Sin, Justification, the Sacraments of the Holy Mass and the worship of icons.

Contemporary events:
- Luther publishes his 85 theories (1517).
- Charles V is elected emperor (1519).
- Cortez enters Mexico (1519).
- Founding of the order of Jesuits (1534)
- Execution of Tommaso Moro (1535)
- Deceased: Erasmus (1536), Copernicus (1543), Luther (1546).
- Religious peace of Augusta (1555)
- Charles V abdicates the throne.
- Michelangelo starts St. Peter's cupola (1546), the largest in the world.

The Trent Cathedral where the longest council in history was held: 18 years.

20°
FIRST VATICAN COUNCIL

1869 A.D.
December 8, 1869 - October 20, 1870

POPE
PIUS IX (255)

PAPAL BULL
"Aeterni Patris"

The council was summoned to the Vatican, by Pius IX and was attended by 700 bishops. The infallibility of the Pope speaking "ex-cathedra" as shepherd of the Christians and Father of the Church was established. The Council was delayed "sine die" due to the Italian troops occupying Rome on September 20, 1870.

Contemporary events:
- End of the American Civil War (1865)
- Opening of the Suez Canal (1869)
- French-Prussian war (1870-1871)
- End of the "Pontifical State". Rome becomes the capital of Italy (September 20, 1870)

St. Peter's square on opening day of the First Vatican Council.

21°
SECOND VATICAN COUNCIL

1962 A.D.
October 11, 1962 to December 8, 1965

POPE
JOHN XXIII (261)
PAUL VI (262)

PAPAL BULL
"Humanae Salutis"

This Council is considered to be the most important in the history of the Church: 2450 Conciliar Fathers from all over the world were present. These Ecumenical Council was conceived by Pope John XXIII, "The Good Pope", the Parish Priest of the world who envisioned a universal catholic assembly.

Particular characteristics of the Council were: attitude of conciliation and openness towards the separate Christian churches; increased secular participation in the life of the Church; strengthening of the privileges of the episcopacy in a collective manner; change in the sacred liturgy by replacing Latin with the local language; freedom for men to profess their own personal religious convictions and the unlawfulness of any form of external coercion to impede it; condemnation of any form of racial discrimination; respect of the church for all religions and exhortation of the Christians to speak and co-operate with the followers of other religion; respect for all that is holy and true in Hinduism and Buddhism; Islamic belief in a single God; acknowledgment of Christ as a prophet, veneration of the Virgin Mary, awaiting of the final judgment and resurrection, value of the judgment and resurrection, value of prayer, charity and fasting; establish that men are called to forget all grudges in the spirit of mutual brotherly understanding; establish that Jewish people cannot be classified, scolded or cursed as killers of God, neither present-day nor ancient Hebrews may be accused of the death of Christ.

The sentences of excommunication between the Pontifical Legates and the patriarchs and the Synod of Constantinople, which caused distressful events in 1054, were to be disapproved and obliterated.

Contemporary events:
- Use of atomic energy.
- Human exploration of outer space.
- Emancipation of the Asian and African peoples.
- Strategic alliance of the western countries (NATO).
- The church altar is turned toward the faithful for the celebration of Mass in local languages.

Miniature of the indiction Bull "Humanae Salutis" for the Second Vatican Council. The symbols of the vine, laurel, wheat and palm are indicative of the youth of the Church "Ego Sum Vitis", of peace and the Eucharistic bread.

FROM THE FIRST JUBILEE IN 1300 TO THE HOLY YEAR OF 2000

History of 28 Jubilees

The bronze Holy Door of St. Peter's Basilica that changed a centuries old tradition for the Holy Year's opening and closing ceremony (see Holy Years XXV, XXVI and XXVII).

"DE JUBILEO"

Origin of the Jubilee

God established, through the help of his servant Moses, three institutions for the Jewish people: first institution was that on the seventh day of the week, Saturday (the day of the Lord), was to be dedicated to God, rest and prayer; the second institution was that a sabbatical year (every seven years) was intended to remind man that God is the only master of the world; the third institution, the year of the Jubilee (the last year of the seventh seven-year period, corresponding to the fiftieth year) was established to be a moment when all material goods were to be returned, slaves freed and debts forgiven.

This year was called the Jubilee year from "the Year of the Yobel" (Year of the Ram's Horn) because it was proclaimed by the blast of horns.

With the advent of the gospel, i.e. the announcement of the coming and glory of Christ, Moses' institutions no longer had the same significance, and acquired new meaning, because the prophecy of the coming of the Messiah had been fulfilled with the birth of Jesus.

Year One of the Christian Era:

Sunday became the day of rest and prayer in remembrance of Jesus' resurrection (Sunday, from the Latin "Dominus", meaning day of the Lord). The Christian Church abolished the sabbatical year as well as the last year of the seventh seven-year period.

The laws governing material goods in the Jewish Jubilee were applied by the Christian church in more spiritual terms.

The Jubilee in Rome

Boniface VIII established the recurrence of the Jubilee which would give devout Christians a specific amount of time in which to fully examine their conscience and soul; before this time, other Popes had attempted to establish specific periods for the forgiveness of sins but the periods and the conditions governing them were always different.

The Jubilean period of forgiveness was deeply felt by the faithful and, as a result, the successive Popes decided to repeat the plenary indulgence, granted by Boniface VIII, at regular intervals. The Jubilee, called the Holy Year since 1500, is a time for total forgiveness and the granting plenary remission of all sins.

I
HUNDREDTH OF INDULGENCE
1350

BONIFACE VIII

- **Proclaimed and celebrated** by Boniface VIII, born Benedetto Caetani in the Lazio region. Elected December 24, 1294 - died October 10, 1303.
- **Papal Bull** of February 22, 1300: *ANTIQUORUM HABET DIGNA FIDE RELATIO*
- **Started** Feb. 22, 1300 (feast day of "St. Peter's chair").
- **Ended** Christmas Eve 1300.
- There were no special Jubilean entrances.
- **Visits** to St. Peter's and S. Paolo's Basilicas for indulgence.

II
YEAR OF THE JUBILEE
1350

CLEMENT VI

- **Proclaimed and celebrated** by Clement VI, born Pietro Roger, from France. Elected May 19, 1342 in Avignon - died December 6, 1352.
- **Papal Bull** of January 27, 1343: *UNIGENITUS DEI FILIUS*
- **Jubilean interval** reduced to 50 years.
- **Started** December 24, 1349.
- **Ended** December 24, 1350.
- There were no special Jubilean entrances.
- **Jubilean visits** to St. Peter's and St. Paolo's Basilicas and, from this point onward, to St. Giovanni.

Tiara of Pope Pius XI. The first crown, representing spiritual power, worn by Pope Sergious II (904). The second crown, added by Boniface VIII (1294), represented royal power. The third crown, added by Urban V (1362), represented temporal power (which ended with Pius IX in 1870). Pope Paul VI was the last to be crowned with the tiara.

The 122-step staircase leading to the church of Santa Maria of Aracoeli at the Capitol Hill was built for the Jubilee of 1350. A memorial tablet was placed on the facade.

III
YEAR OF THE JUBILEE
1390

URBAN VI

BONIFACE IX

- **Proclaimed** by Urban VI, born Bartolomeo Prignano, in the Campania region.
  Elected in the Vatican on April 18, 1378 died October 15, 1389.
- **Papal Bull** of April 8, 1389:
  SALVATOR NOSTER UNIGENITUS DEI FILIUS
- Jubilean recurrence shortened to 33 years.

- **Confirmed and celebrated** by Boniface IX, born Pietro Tomacelli, in the Campania region.
  Elected in the Vatican on November 9, 1389 died October 1, 1404.
- **Papal Bull** of June 11, 1390:
  DUDUM FELICIS
- **Started** December 24, 1389
- **Ended** December 24, 1390
- No special Jubilean entrances
- **Jubilean visits** to the four Patriarchal Basilicas: St. Peter's, San Giovanni's, San Paolo's and, from this Jubilee onward, Santa Maria Maggiore.

The reduced interval between Jubilees, from 50 to 35 years, was decided by Urban VI and confirmed by Boniface IX. This Jubilee should have been celebrated in 1383; it was delayed because the Pope was away from Rome due to a severe outbreak of the plague. This Jubilee was the first extraordinary of the "Redemption".

Santa Maria Maggiore is the fourth Patriarchal Basilica. At this time, the Basilica was outside of the city, in the countryside, on the Esquiline Hill. The Pope chose it as his summer residence.

BONIFACE IX

MARTIN V

- **Confirmed and celebrated** by Boniface IX, born Pietro Tomacelli, in the Campania region.
  Elected in the Vatican on November 9, 1389 died October 1, 1404.
- **Papal Bull** was not issued
- Centenary Jubilean recurrence
- **Started** at the end of 1399 without ceremonies
- **Ended** December 24, 1400
- No special Jubilean entrances
- **Jubilean visits** to the four Patriarchal Basilicas, plus San Lorenzo Fuori le Mura, Santa Maria in Trastevere and, only for this year, Santa Maria Rotonda (Pantheon).

- **Proclaimed and celebrated** by Martin V, born Oddone Colonna in the Lazio Region, elected November 21, 1417 died February 20, 1431
- **Papal Bull:** the document was never found.
- 33 year Jubilean interval recurrence was resumed (see 1390).
- **Started** December 21, 1422
- **Ended** December 24, 1423
- The first Jubilean entrance was consecrated in the Basilica of San Giovanni.
- Visits to the other three Patriarchal Basilicas.

The Basilica of S. Lorenzo Fuori le Mura was also included for Jubilean visits. The mosaics on the facade, made by S. Capparoni in 1864, were destroyed during the bombings on July 19, 1943.

Pope Martin V established the first Jubilean entrance at the Basilica of S. Giovanni in Laterano; the entrance was later called "Holy Door" (1500). The small door jambs seen in the picture are from the ancient Constantine's Basilica.

VI
YEAR OF THE JUBILEE
1450

NICHOLAS V

- **Proclaimed and celebrated** by Nicholas V, born Tommaso Perentucelli in the Liguria region, elected February 19, 1447 - died March 24, 1455.
- **Papal Bull** of January 19, 1449:
  IMMENSA ET INNUMERABILIA
- *Jubilean interval* recurrence was reinstated at every 50 years (see 1350)
- **Started** December 24, 1449
- *Ended* December 24, 1450
- Jubilean entrance only at S. Giovanni's Basilica and visits.

In the medieval tabernacle of San Giovanni's Basilica, the heads of St. Peter and St. Paul are preserved in silver reliquaries. During the Jubilee, the relics were put on display for the pilgrims and could even be touched.

VII
YEAR OF THE JUBILEE
1475

PAUL II

SIXTUS IV

- **Willed and established** by Paul II, born Pietro Barbo from Venice.
  Elected September 16, 1464 - died July 26, 1471.
- **Jubilean recurrence** every 25 years
- **Papal Bull** of April 19, 1470:
  INNEFABILI PROVIDENTIA SUMMI PATRIS
- **Proclaimed and celebrated** by Sixtus IV, born Francesco della Rovere in the Liguria region. Elected August 25, 1471 - died August 12, 1484.
- **Papal Bull** of August 29, 1473
  Salvator noster
- Jubilean interval confirmed at 25 years
- **Started** December 24, 1474
- **Ended** Easter 1476
- Jubilean entrance only at S. Giovanni's Basilica and visits.

Corrado Sweinhein and Arnaldo Pannartz, German cleric printers living in Subiaco, were invited by Paul II to come to work in Rome. The first printed Italian book "History of Christ's Passion" was printed in Subiaco in 1462. The first book on "Ecclesiastical Indulgences" was printed during this Jubilee. The "History and Description of Rome" was the first tourist guide to be published.

VIII HOLY YEAR
OF THE JUBILEE
1500

ALEXANDER VI

- **Proclaimed and celebrated** by Alexander VI, born Rodrigo de Borja in Spain. Elected August 26, 1492 - died August 18, 1503 (possibly due to pestilence).
- **Papal Bull** of March 28, 1499
  INTER CAUSAS MULTIPLICES
- **Started** December 24, 1499
- **Ended** January 6, 1501
- Jubilean Holy Doors open in the four Patriarchal Basilicas.

From this Jubilee onward, the time for total forgiveness is called Holy Year and the plenary indulgence is granted by entering through the Holy Door.

In the drawing, the ancient façade of Constantine's Basilica. The Holy Door(*). The obelisk of Nero's Circus, on the left, is presently found in St. Peter's Square. On the right, the roof of the Sistine Chapel.

IX HOLY YEAR
OF THE JUBILEE
1525

CLEMENT VII

- **Proclaimed and celebrated** by Clement VII, born Giulio de' Medici in the Toscana Region. Elected November 26, 1523 - died September 25, 1534.
- **Papal Bull** of December. 17, 1524
  INTER SOLLECITUDINES ET CORAM NOBIS
- **Started** December 24, 1524
- **Ended** December 24, 1525
- Holy Doors and visits to the four Patriarchal Basilicas.

The medal in memory of the opening of the Holy Door was made in the second half of the 18th century by Girolamo Paladino.
For the first time in history Clement VII had an official coin minted to commemorate the Jubilee, with the Holy Door being depicted on the coin.

X HOLY YEAR OF THE JUBILEE 1550

PAUL III

JULIUS III

- **Called** by Paul III, born Alessandro Farnese in the Lazio region.
  Elected October 3, 1534 - died November 10, 1549.

- **Proclaimed and celebrated** by Julius III, born Giovanni Maria Ciocchi del Monte in Rome.
  Elected on February 22, 1550 - died March 23, 1555.
- **Papal Bull** of February 10, 1550
  SI PASTORE OVIUM
- **Started** February 24, 1550
- **Ended** January 6, 1551
- Holy Doors and visits to the four Patriarchal Basilicas.

Michelangelo's definitive project for the Capitol and his Palaces. The geometrically designed floor was finally realized in 1940 under Governor Prince Giacomo Borghese.

XI HOLY YEAR OF THE JUBILEE 1575

GREGORY VIII

- **Proclaimed and celebrated** by Gregory XIII, born Ugo Boncompagni in the Emilia region.
  Elected May 25, 1572 - died April 10, 15
- **Papal Bull** of May 20, 1574 (Ascension Day)
  DOMINUS AC REDEMPTOR NOSTER JESUS
- **Started** December 24, 1574
- **Ended** December 24, 1575
- Holy Doors in the four Patriarchal basilicas and, from this Holy Year onward, visits to S. Sebastiano (Catacombs), S. Lorenzo Fuori le Mura and Santa Croce in Jerusalem in Rome.

Roman catacombs were generally used to bury the dead during the persecution of the Christians. St. Sebastian's Cemetery, situated on the Appian Way, was excavated on four levels. Many prayers scratched on the walls prove that the bodies of the Apostles Peter and Paul were preserved in this cemetery since the third century.

XII HOLY YEAR
OF THE JUBILEE
1600

CLEMENT VIII

- **Proclaimed and celebrated** by Clement VIII, born Ippolito Aldobrandini in the Marche region. Elected February 9, 1592 - died March 3, 1605.
- **Papal Bull** of May 19, 1599:
  ANNUS DOMINI PLACABILIS
- **Started** December 31, 1599
- **Ended** January 13, 1601
- Holy Doors in the four Patriarchal Basilicas and visits as in the XI Jubilee (1575).

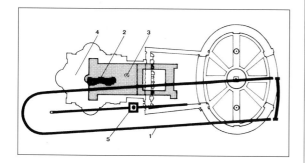

The pilgrims of this Holy Year found the Egyptian monolithic obelisk removed from Nero's Circus and transferred to St. Peter's Square.
1. Nero's Circus - 2. The necropolis where the tomb of St. Peter is found - 3. Basilica of the Emperor Constantine - 4. Present-day Basilica - 5. Obelisk of the Pharaoh Sesostri (2000 B.C.).

XIII HOLY YEAR
OF THE JUBILEE
1625

URBAN VIII

- **Proclaimed and celebrated** by Urban VIII, born Maffeo Barberini in the Toscana region. Elected September 29, 1623 - died July 29, 1644
- **Papal Bull** of April 29, 1624.
  OMNES GENTES PLAUDITE MANIBUS
- **Started** December 24, 1624
- **Ended** December 24, 1625
- Holy Doors to the four Patriarchal Basilicas and visits.

Because of the overflow dread of the Tiber, that could have isolated San Paolo's Basilica, Urban VIII established the church of S. Maria in Trastevere as a Jubilean church with the central door as the Holy Door. S. Maria in Trastevere was chosen because it was the first church in Rome opened by St. Callistus in 221.

XIV YEAR
OF THE JUBILEE
1650

INNOCENT X

- Proclaimed and celebrated by Innocent X, born Giovanni Battista Pamphili in the Lazio region. Elected October 4, 1644 - died January 7, 1655.
- **Papal Bull** of May 4, 1649:
  APPROPINQUANT DILECTISSIMI FILII
- **Started** December 24, 1649
- **Ended** December 24, 1650.
- Holy Doors in the four Patriarchal Basilicas and visits as in the XI Jubilee (1575).

Bernini was appointed to the restoration of the patriarchal basilicas for the upcoming Jubilee. The stone floor in St. Peter's was removed and substituted with a polychromatic marble design and completed on September 25, 1649. The floor of the central nave has brass plates set in it that carry the comparative length of other great churches around the world.

XV HOLY YEAR
OF THE JUBILEE
1675

CLEMENT X

- **Proclaimed and celebrated** by Clement X, born Emilio Altieri in Rome. Elected May 11, 1670 - died July 22, 1676.
- **Papal Bull** of April 16, 1674
  AD APOSTOLICAE VOCIS ORACULUM
- **Started** December 24, 1674
- **Ended** December 24, 1675
- Holy Doors and visits as in the XI Jubilee.

The pilgrims of this Jubilee found St. Angelo's Bridge adorned with ten marble angels. Each angel represents a symbol of Christ's passion. Bernini designed the angels that were sculpted by his students.

XVI HOLY YEAR OF THE JUBILEE 1700

INNOCENT XII

CLEMENT XI

- **Proclaimed and opened** by Innocent XII, born Antonio Pignatelli in the Puglia region.
  Elected July 15, 1691 - died September 27, 1700.
- **Papal Bull** of May 18, 1669:
  REGI SAECULORUM
- **Started** December 24, 1699

- **Celebrated** by Clement XI, born Gian Francesco Albani in the Marche region. Elected November 30, 1700- died March 19, 1721.
- **Closed** December 24, 1700.
- Holy Doors in the three Patriarchal Basilicas, with the exception of St. Paolo's (see: XIII Jubilee-1625) and visits as in the XI Jubilee.

The artistically engraved hammer head used by Innocent XII for the opening ceremony of St. Peter's Holy Door.

XVII HOLY YEAR OF THE JUBILEE 1725

BENEDICT XIII

- **Proclaimed and celebrated** by Benedict XIII, born Pietro Francesco (Vincenzo Maria) Orsini in the Puglia region.
  Elected June 4, 1724 - died February 21, 1730.
- **Papal Bull** of June 26, 1724:.
  REDEMPTOR ET DOMINUS NOSTER JESUS CHRISTUS
- **Started** December 24, 1724
- **Ended** December 24, 1725
- Holy Doors in the four Patriarchal Basilicas and visits as in the XI Jubilee (1575).

The staircase at Trinità dei Monti, a major architectural project of the 1700's, was designed by F. De Sanctis, by order of Benedict XIII. The staircase, divided in five ramps of 12 steps each, took only three years to complete.

XVIII HOLY YEAR OF THE JUBILEE 1750

BENEDICT XIV

- **Proclaimed and celebrated** by Benedict XIV, born Prospero Lambertini in the Emilia region. Elected August 22, 1740- died April 3, 1758.
- **Papal Bull** of May 5, 1749
PEREGRINANTES A DOMINO
- **Started** December 24, 1749
- **Ended** December 24, 1750
- Holy Doors in the four Patriarchal Basilicas and visits as in the XI Jubilee (1575).

Leonard from Porto Maurizio (Oneglia), while studying in Rome, was miraculously healed from a serious sickness. After this event, he became a preacher and Benedict XIV, touched by his words, appointed him to prepare this Jubilee. Leonard started the tradition of the "Via Crucis" at the Coliseum by walking and standing barefoot while preaching in front of the 14 Stations of the Cross. In 1929, after the reconciliation, the Cross was moved to the north side of the auditorium.

XIX HOLY YEAR OF THE JUBILEE 1775

CLEMENT XIV

PIUS VI

- **Proclaimed** by Clement XIV, born Giovanni Vincenzo Ganganelli in the Romagna region. Elected April 28, 1769 - died September 22, 1774.
- **Papal Bull** of April 30, 1774
SALUTIS NOSTRAE AUCTOR

- **Celebrated** by Pius VI, born Giovanni Angelo Braschi of the Romagna Region. Elected February 22, 1775 - died August 29, 1799.
- **Papal Bull,** confirming Clemente XIV's bull, published in Italian
"THE AUTHOR OF OUR HEALTH"
- **Started** February 26, 1775 (because of the Vacancy of the See)
- **Ended** December 31, 1775
- Holy Doors in the four Patriarchal Basilicas and visits as in the XI Jubilee (1575).

On November 30, 1775, as per tradition, Pope Pius VI, followed by the Pontifical Court, rode on horseback to S. Giovanni in Laterano where he took possession of the cathedral as Bishop of Rome.

HOLY YEAR
OF THE JUBILEE
1800

PIUS VII

- **Neither proclaimed nor celebrated** by Pius VII, born Gregorio Barnaba Chiaramonti in the Romagna region.
  Elected March 14, 1800- died August 20, 1823
- **Encyclical** of May 24, 1800:
  EX QUO ECCLESIAM
- **The Holy Doors were not opened.**

Main events that kept the Holy Year from being celebrated in 1800.

1796 - The French revolution starts. Napoleon, together with his army, occupies Northern Italy and seizes Romagna from the Papal State.
1797 - After long resistance Pope Pius VI is forced to sign the Treaty of Tolentino.
1798 - The Republic of Tiber is proclaimed inside the Papal State and Pius VI is arrested.
1799 - August 29: Pope Pius VI dies in Valence (France).
1800 - March 14: After a six-month vacancy of the See, Pope Pius VII is elected in Venice and arrives in Rome on July 3rd.
1801 - By order of Napoleon, the mortal remains of Pius VI are sent back to the Vatican where they arrive on Christmas Eve.
1804 - November 2: Pope Pius VII is forced to crown Napoleon in France.
1808 - Rome is occupied by Napoleon's Army.
1809 - Napoleon decrees the end of the Pontiff's Dominion and on July 6th Pope Pius VII is arrested and taken to France.
1814 - Napoleon's fortunes decline. Bonaparte resides at Elba.
1815 - After the Battle of Waterloo, Napoleon is exiled to the island of St. Helen.
1820 - The Secret Society of the Risorgimento, "the Carbonari", rebels against the northern and southern Italian governments.
1823 - On August 8th, Pope Pius VII dies as a result of a bad fall. The Basilica of S. Paolo goes up in flames.

After the reinstatement of temporal power in 1815, Pope Pius VII changes the Papal State flag colours from yellow and deep red, the colours originally attributed to Rome, to yellow and white.

XX HOLY YEAR
OF THE JUBILEE
1825

LEO XII

- **Proclaimed and celebrated** by Leo XII, born Annibale Sermattei della Genga in the Marche region. Elected September 28, 1823 - died February 10, 1829.
- **Papal Bull** of May 24, 1824.
  QUOD HOC INEUNTE SAECULO
- **Started** December 24, 1824
- **Ended** December 24, 1825
- Holy Doors in three Patriarchal Basilicas and visits as in the XI Jubilee (1575).

St. Paul's Basilica was almost totally destroyed by a fire on the night of July 15, 1823. A candle that was left burning by the restoration crews ignited a fire on the roof. The news never reached Pius VII who died a month later. The Basilica was reconstructed and reconsecrated in 1854. The facade's polychromatic mosaics were made by Agricola and Consoni in 1874.

H0LY YEAR OF THE JUBILEE 1850

PIUS IX

- **Neither proclaimed nor celebrated** by Pius IX, born Giovanni Maria Mastai Ferretti in the Marche region.
  Elected June 21, 1846 - died February 7, 1878.
- **Sacred invitation,** June 17, 1850
- **Period** of indulgence from June 19 to July 9.
- **The holy doors were not opened.**

Main events that kept the 1850 Holy Year from being celebrated.
Revolts of the Risorgimento and Independence Wars in Italy and Europe.
1848 - Nov 15: Pellegrino Rossi, Police Headmaster of the Pontifical State, was assassinated. Roman problems worsened.
1848 - Nov 24: Pope Pius IX took refuge in Gaeta, Kingdom of the Bourbons.
1849 - Feb 9: Rome had neither sovereign nor government. The Constituent Assembly was convoked. For the third time during this century the end of Pontifical Temporal Power was declared. The Roman Republic was established and proclaimed.
1849 - April 25: 7 000 French soldiers, called to help by the Pope, disembarked at Civitavecchia's Pontifical harbor.
1849 - April 30: fighting outside the walls at St. Pancrazio's door. Commander Oudinot lost the battle and asked for armistice until the 4th of June. April 31st the armistice was signed, the hostilities ended on May 7.
1849 - Bargaining continued between the Roman Republic and the French ambassador Ferdinand-Marie de Lesseps.
1849 - June 3: Commander Oudinot, with a reinforcement of French troops (36 000 soldiers and 36 cannons), surprised the republicans by starting a battle during the night.
1849 - June 30: after 20 days of cannonades, with the bastions destroyed, the French won against the exhausted Republicans' resistance.
1849 - July 3: the terms of surrender of the Roman Republic were signed.
1850 - April 12: Pope Pius IX returned to the Vatican.

XXI HOLY YEAR OF THE JUBILEE 1875

PIUS IX

- **Proclaimed and celebrated** by Pius IX, born Giovanni Maria Mastai Ferretti in the Marche region. Elected June 21, 1846 - died February 7, 1878. (See 1850 Jubilee)
- **Papal Bull** of December 24, 1874.
  GRAVIBUS ECCLESIAE SED SAECULI CALAMITATIS
- **Started** January 1, 1875
- **Ended** December 31, 1875
- **Holy Doors where not opened, visits only.**

Pius IX, after the fall of the Pontifical State in 1877, became a voluntary prisoner. For the 50th anniversary of his ordination as Bishop of Spoleto, he received hundreds of gifts. Even Vittorio Emanuele II, King of Italy, gave him a very original wooden throne covered with original Gobelins tapestry. See detail of the House of Savoy coat of arms on the front lower cross-bar.

XXII HOLY YEAR OF THE JUBILEE 1900

LEO XIII

- **Proclaimed and celebrated** by Leo XIII, born Vincenzo Gioacchino Pecci in the Lazio region. Elected March 3, 1878 - died July 20, 1903.
- **Papal Bull** of May 11, 1899:
  PROPERANTE AD EXITUM SAECULO
- **Started** December 24, 1899
- **Ended** December 24, 1900.
- Holy Doors in the four Patriarchal Basilica and visits as in the XI Jubilee (1575).

The ceremony of the lowering of the brick wall using a series of pulleys, depicted by the artist Dante Paolocci for the magazine "Illustrazione Italiana".

XXIII HOLY YEAR OF THE JUBILEE 1925

PIUS XI

- **Proclaimed and celebrated** by Pius XI, born Achille Ratti in the Lombardia Region. Elected February 12, 1922 died February 10, 1939.
- **Papal Bull** of May 29, 1924:
  INFINITA DEI MISERICORDIA
- **Started** December 24, 1924
- **Ended** December 24, 1925
- Holy Doors in the four Patriarchal Basilicas and visits; same as in the XI Jubilee (1575).

An incredible sight. The main contours of the Basilica façade and the cupola are lit by hundreds of tallow-torches. Young experienced "sampietrini" used to lower a long rope from the cupola to the façade to light the torches one at a time. The torches on the Cross situated at top of the cupola, measuring 139 meters from the ground, were lit with the help of a small external iron ladder belonging to the cupola.

XXIV HOLY YEAR OF THE JUBILEE 1933

PIUS XI

- **Extraordinary** because proclaimed outside of the twenty-five year rule (extraordinem)
- **Proclaimed and celebrated** by Pius XI, born Achille Ratti in the Lombardia Region. Elected February 12, 1922 - died February 10, 1939. **"First of the Redention"**
- **Papal Bull** of January 6, 1933: *QUOD NUPER*
- **Started** April 1, 1933 (Easter Saturday)
- **Ended** April 2, 1934 (Easter Monday)
- Holy Doors and visits to the 4 patriarchal Basilicas, S. Croce in Jerusalem, S. Lorenzo and S. Sebastiano (Catacombs).

"Via della Conciliazione" named after the historic reconciliation between the Holy See and Italy called the Lateran Treaty because the documents were signed in the Popes' hall at the Lateran Palace, once a Pontiff's residence. The three Treaty documents, the Political Treaty, Convention and Concordat, were signed by Cardinal Pietro Gasbarri and Benito Mussolini, on February 12, 1929, 30 months after the negotiations had started. Finally, after 60 years the "Roman Issue" was resolved.

XXV HOLY YEAR OF THE JUBILEE 1950

PIUS XII

- **Proclaimed and celebrated** by Pius XII, born Eugenio Pacelli in Rome. Elected March 12, 1939 - died Oct 9, 1958.
- **Papal Bull** of May 26, 1949: *JUBILAEUM MAXIMUM*
- **Started** December 24, 1949
- **Ended** December 24, 1950
- Holy Doors in the four Patriarchal Basilicas and visits as in the XI Jubilee (1575).

In the 1950 Jubilee a bronze door was commissioned and installed for the purpose of keeping the Jubilean entrance closed at night. At the end of the Holy Year, the brick walls were erected for the last time (see 1975 Jubilee) and the bronze door was placed against the interior brick wall.

XXVI HOLY YEAR
OF THE JUBILEE
1975

PAUL VI

- **Proclaimed and celebrated** by Paul VI, born Giovanni Battista Montini of Lombardy. Elected June 21, 1963 - died August 6, 1978.
- **Papal Bull** of May 23, 1974: *APOSTOLORUM LIMINA*
- **Started** December 24, 1974
- **Ended** December 24, 1975
- Holy Doors in the four Patriarchal Basilicas and visits as in the XI Jubilee (1575)

This was the last Holy Year with the traditional opening of demolishing the brick wall. After an incident that occurred at the opening ceremony a decision was taken to close the Holy Door, at the end of the Jubilee, with only the bronze door made by Vico Consorti.

XXVII HOLY YEAR
OF THE JUBILEE
1983

JOHN PAUL II

- **Extraordinary** because proclaimed outside of the twenty-five year rule (extraordinem)

- **Proclaimed and celebrated** by John Paul II, born Karol Wojtyla in Poland. Elected October 16, 1978 and still reigning.
  "Second of the Redemption"
- **Papal Bull** of January 6, 1983 *APERITE PORTAS REDEMPTORI*
- **Started** March 25, 1983 - April 22, 1984
- Holy Doors and visits as in the XI Jubilee (1575)

This is the first Jubilee where the Holy Door is opened after three knocks but without the traditional demolition of the brick wall.

XXVIII HOLY YEAR
OF THE GREAT JUBILEE
2000

JOHN PAUL II

- **Proclaimed** by John Paul II, born Karol Wojtyla in Poland.
  Elected on October 16, 1978.
  Papal Bull of November 29, 1998:
  INCARNATIONIS MYSTERIUM
- **Starts** December 24, 1999 - Friday
  Opening of the St. Peter's Holy Door
  Solemn Mass at midnight
  December 25, 1999 - Saturday
  Opening of the Holy Doors in the Basilicas of San Giovanni in Laterano and Santa Maria Maggiore.
  Mid-day mass at St. Peter's and "Urbi et Orbi" Blessing.
  Opening of the Jubilee in the Holy Land and Local Churches.
  January 18, 2000 - Tuesday
  Opening of the Holy Door in the Basilica of San Paolo Fuori le Mura.

Ends January 5, 2001 - Thursday
Closing of the Holy Doors in the Basilicas of San Giovanni in Laterano, Santa Maria Maggiore and San Paolo Fuori le Mura.
End of the Jubilee in the Holy Land and Local Churches.
January 6, 2001 - Friday
Closing of the Holy Door in the St. Peter's Basilica.

BIMILLENARY CELEBRATION OF THE MYSTERY OF CHRIST

Since Jerusalem and other Holy Sites became difficult to visit, due to ancient historical problems, Rome became the principal destination for pilgrims. They come to Rome for the Apostle's memories, for the testimonials of many martyrs and for Peter's successor: the Holy Father and Bishop of Rome.

In the year 2000, the first Jubilee of the telematic era and social universal communications will witness the coming of pilgrims from all over the world in the name of the plurality of nations and the triple ecumenical realities. First, the Liturgical celebrations will culminate on Easter day, April 23, 2000, Christmas day, December 25, 2000 and the Epiphany, January 6, 2001. Second, the Jubilean reality, consisting in the traditional penitential celebrations of the Holy Years. Third, the Ecclesiastical reality promulgated in the Apostolic Letter "Tertio Millennio Adveniente" (November 10th, 1994), describing Church events and international commemorations.

For the first time, the Great Jubilee will be celebrated simultaneously in the Holy Land, Rome and local churches around the world. For the Jubilee of the year 2000, celebrations will be held in all different liturgical rites: Syro-Eastern (January 28 in S. Cecilia in Trastevere), Syro-Antiochian (Maronite, February 9 in S. Maria Maggiore), Alexandrian (May 26 in S. Maria degli Angeli), Coptic (August 14 in S. Maria Maggiore), Armenian and Antasdan (September 14 in S. Croce in Gerusalemme), Byzantine (October 1st in S. Maria sopra Minerva), Ambrosian (November 4 ....), Syro-Antiochian (Syrians and Malankarenians in S. Maria in Trastevere), Mozarabic (December 16 in S. Maria Maggiore).

Printed October 1999 by
Euroedit s.r.l. - Trento
Via del Commercio, 59
Ph. 0641.822521 - 827095

Filmsetting by Graf Art - Trento
Photoreproduction by Artilitho - Trento